Carrying on in Key S...

Providing continuity in purposeful play and exploration

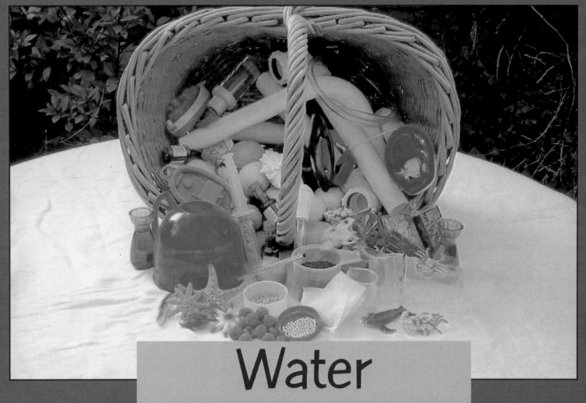

Water

Ros Bayley, Lynn Broadbent, Sally Featherstone

Carrying on in Key Stage 1

Water

ISBN 1 906029 13 x   •   978 1 906029 13 5

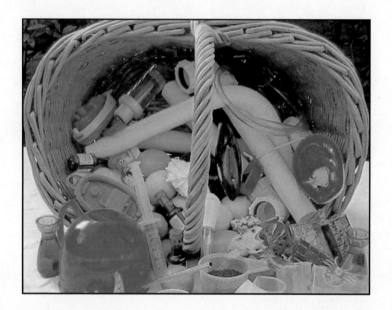

Featherstone Education Ltd
44-46 High Street
Husbands Bosworth
Leicestershire
LE17 6LP

www.featherstone.uk.com

First published in the UK, May 2007

Printed in the United Kingdom on paper produced in the European Union from managed, sustainable forests.

Contents

Carrying on in Key Stage One

This series of books is intended to support the continuing growth and development of independent learning and practical activities, which are key features of the Early Years Foundation Stage.

Children in Key Stage One need and deserve the chance to build on the best of practice in the Early Years Foundation Stage, which carefully balances adult directed tasks with learning that children initiate and develop themselves, often in the company of responsive adults. These activities, which include sand and water play, construction, role play, independent mark making and writing, creative work, dance and movement, and outdoor play, are some of the activities children value most and miss most in Years One and Two.

> Parent: 'What's it like in Year 1?'
>
> Child: 'There en't no sand and the work's too 'ard.'

This quote from a Year 1 boy echoes the feelings of many children who need to continue the learning styles and situations offered in Reception classes. However, many teachers in Key Stage One feel intense pressure to concentrate on activities that require recording and increasing levels of direction by adults. Why is this, and is it right for teachers to feel so pressured?

One thing we know from research is that practical activity and independent learning are essential for brain growth and reinforcement of growing abilities throughout childhood, at least till the onset of puberty, and for many children this is a lifelong need. We also know that the embedding of learning and the transformation of this into real understanding takes time and practice. Skills need to be reinforced by revisiting them in many different contexts in child initiated learning, and practical challenges, and practical tasks in real life situations will be far more effective than rote learning, worksheets or adult direction.

> 'I hear and I forget,
>
> I see and I remember,
>
> I do and I understand.'
>
> Ancient Chinese Proverb

EVERY CHILD MATTERS
The five outcomes:
Enjoy and achieve
Stay safe
Be healthy
Make a positive contribution
Achieve economic well-being

It is also clear from brain research that many boys (and some girls) are just not ready by the end of Reception to embark on a formal curriculum which involves a lot of sitting down, listening and writing. Their bodies and their brains still need action, challenge and freedom to explore materials and resources in freedom.

But this does not mean that challenge should be absent from such activity! The brain feeds on challenge and novelty, so teachers and other adults working in Key Stage One need to structure the experiences, so they build on existing skills and previous activities, while presenting new opportunities to explore familiar materials in new and exciting ways. Such challenges and activities can:

- ♦ be led by the Programme of Study for Key Stage One;
- ♦ focus on thinking skills and personal capabilities;
- ♦ relate to real world situations and stimuli;
- ♦ help children to achieve the five outcomes for Every Child Matters.

In Carrying on in Key Stage 1, we aim to give you the rationale, the process and the confidence to continue a practical, child centred curriculum which also helps you as teachers to recognise the requirements of the statutory curriculum for Key Stage One. Each book in the series follows the same format, and addresses objectives from many areas of the National Curriculum. Of course, when children work on practical challenges, curriculum elements become intertwined, and many will be going on simultaneously.

The Role of the Adult

Of course, even during child initiated learning, the role of the adult is crucial. Sensitive adults play many roles as they support, challenge and engage the children in their care. High quality teaching is not easy! If teachers want to expand experiences and enhance learning, they need to be able to stand back, to work alongside, and extend or scaffold the children's learning by offering provocations and challenges to their thinking and activity. The diagram below attempts to describe this complex task, and the way that adults move around the elements in the circle of learning. For ease of reading we have described the elements in the following way, and each double page spread covers all three of the vital roles adults play.

Recognising and building on the practical activities which children have experienced before

This element of the process is vital in scaffolding children's learning so it makes sense to them. Your knowledge of the Foundation Stage curriculum and the way it is organised will be vital in knowing where to start. Teachers and other adults should have first hand knowledge of both the resources and the activities which have been available and how they have been offered in both child initiated and adult led activities. This knowledge should be gained by visiting the Reception classes in action, and by talking to adults and children as they work. Looking at Reception planning will also help.

Understanding the range of adult roles, and the effect different roles have on children's learning

Responsive adults react in different ways to what they see and hear during the day. This knowledge will influence the way they plan for further experiences which meet emerging needs and build on individual interests. The diagram illustrates the complex and interlinking ways in which adults interact with children's learning. Observing, co-playing and extending learning often happen simultaneously, flexibly and sometime unconsciously. It is only when we reflect on our work with children that we realise what a complex and skilled activity is going on.

Offering challenges and provocations

As the adults collect information about the learning, they begin to see how they can help children to extend and scaffold their thinking and learning. The adults offer challenges or provocations which act like grit in an oyster, provoking the children to produce responses and think in new ways about what they know and can do.

Linking the learning with the skills and content of the curriculum

As the children grapple with new concepts and skills, adults can make direct links with curriculum intentions and content. These links can be mapped out across the range of knowledge, skills and understanding contained in the curriculum guidance for Key Stage One. It is also possible to map the development of thinking skills, personal capabilities and concepts which link the taught curriculum with the real world.

The adult as extender of learning
discusses ideas
shares thinking
makes new possibilities evident
instigates new opportunities for learning
extends and builds on learning and interests
supports children in making links in learning
models new skills and techniques

The adult as co-player
shares responsibility with the child
offers suggestions
asks open questions
responds sensitively
models and imitates
plays alongside

The adult as observer
listens attentively
observes carefully
records professionally
interprets skilfully

Looking for the Learning

As children plan, explore, invent, extend, construct, discuss, question and predict in the rich experiences planned and offered, they will communicate what they are learning through speech and actions, as well as through the outcomes of activities. Assessment for learning involves adults and children in discussing and analysing what they discover. Reflecting on learning, through discussion with other children and adults, is a key factor in securing skills and abilities, fixing and 'hard wiring' the learning in each child's brain. And, of course, teachers and other adults need to recognise, confirm and record children's achievements, both for the self esteem this brings to the children and to fulfil their own duties as educators.

You could find out what children already know and have experienced by:

* talking to them as individuals and in small groups;

* talking to parents and other adults who know them well (teaching assistants are often wonderful sources of information about individual children);

* visiting the Reception classes and looking at spaces, storage and access to resources, including the use of these out of doors;

* providing free access to materials and equipment and watching how children use them when you are not giving any guidance;

* talking as a group or class about what children already know about the materials and those they particularly enjoy using.

Using the curriculum grid to observe, to recognise learning and celebrate achievement

At the end of each section you will find a curriculum grid which covers the whole Programme of Study for Key Stage 1. This is a 'shorthand version' of the full grid included at the end of the book on pages 69-74. A black and white photocopiable version of the grid appears on page 8, so you can make your own copies for planning and particularly for recording observations.

We suggest that as the children work on the provocations and other challenges in this book, adults (teachers and teaching assistants) can use the grid to observe groups of children and record the areas of the curriculum they are covering in their work. The grids can also be used to record what children say and describe in plenary sessions and other discussions.

These observations will enable you to recognise the learning that happens as children explore the materials and engage with the challenging questions you ask and the problems you pose. And of course, as you observe, you will begin to see what needs to happen next; identifying the next steps in learning! This logical and vital stage in the process may identify:

* some children who will be ready for more of the same activity;

* some who need to repeat and reinforce previous stages;

* some who need to relate skills to new contexts, the same activity or skill practiced in a new place or situation;

* some who will want to extend or sustain the current activity in time, space or detail;

* others who will wish to record their work in photos, drawings, models, stories, video etc.

Critical and Thinking Skills

The grid also identifies the key skills which children need for thinking about and evaluating their work. Many schools now observe and evaluate how well these skills are developing when children work on challenging projects and investigations.

> "**Water** is the only substance on earth that is naturally present in three different forms - as a liquid, a solid (ice) and as a gas (water vapour)."
> Unknown

Going Further

Offering extension activities is a way of scaffolding children's learning, taking the known into the unknown, the familiar into the new, the secure into the challenging. It is the role of the adult to turn their knowledge of the children into worthwhile, long term lines of enquiry and development which will become self-sustaining and last throughout life.

At the end of each section in the book you will find a selection of useful resources, links and other information to help you bring construction to life. You could use these resources by encouraging individuals and groups:

* to use the Internet to find images and information;

* to use ICT equipment such as cameras, tape recorders, video and dictaphones to record their explorations and experiments;

* to explore information books in libraries and other places at home and at school;

* to make contact by email and letter with experts, craftsmen, artists, manufacturers, suppliers and other contacts;

* to make books, films, PowerPoint presentations;

* to record their work in photographs and other media;

* to respond to stimuli such as photographs, video, exhibitions and other creative stimuli;

* to look at the built and natural environment with curiosity, interest and creativity;

* to become involved in preserving the natural world, develop environmental awareness and support recycling;

* to look at the world of work and extend their ideas of what they might become and how they might live their lives;

* to develop a sense of economic awareness and the world of work in its widest sense;

* to feel a sense of community and to explore how they might make a contribution to the school and wider communities in which they live;

* to work together and develop the ability to think, reason and solve problems in their learning.

> We recommend that younger children should always work with an adult when accessing search engines and Internet sites.

The suggested resources include websites, books, contacts and addresses. There are also some photographs which may inspire young learners as they work on the provocations and challenges suggested.

We hope you will find the ideas in this book useful in stimulating your work with children in Year 1 and Year 2. The ideas, photos and provocations we have included are only a start to your thinking and exploring together, of course you and the children will have many more as you start to expand the work they do in these practical areas, providing a rich curriculum base using familiar and well loved materials.

If you or the children would like to send us ideas or photographs of the projects inspired by this series, please email us at sally@featherstone.uk.com - we will answer all your messages and put the best ideas on our website.

Ros Bayley, Lynn Broadbent, Sally Featherstone: 2007

Observation of _____ (the activity and resources)

Literacy

Literacy	Lit 1 speak	Lit 2 listen	Lit 3 group	Lit 4 drama	Lit 5 word	Lit 6 spell	Lit 7 text1	Lit 8 text2	Lit 9 text3	Lit10 text4	Lit11 sentence	Lit12 present-ation
	1.1	2.1	3.1	4.1	5.1	6.1	7.1	8.1	9.1	10.1	11.1	12.1
	1.2	2.2	3.2	4.2	5.2	6.2	7.2	8.2	9.2	10.2	11.2	12.2

Numeracy

Numeracy	Num 1 U&A	Num 2 count	Num 3 number	Num 4 calculate	Num 5 shape	Num 6 measure	Num 7 data
	1.1	2.1	3.1	4.1	5.1	6.1	7.1
	1.2	2.2	3.2	4.2	5.2	6.2	7.2

Science

Science	SC1 Enquiry			SC2 Life processes					SC3 Materials		SC4 Phys processes		
	Sc1.1	Sc1.2	Sc1.3	Sc2.1	Sc2.2	Sc2.3	Sc2.4	Sc2.5	Sc3.1	Sc3.2	Sc4.1	Sc4.2	Sc4.3
	1.1a	1.2a	1.3a	2.1a	2.2a	2.3a	2.4a	2.5a	3.1a	3.2a	4.1a	4.2a	4.3a
	1.1b	1.2b	1.3b	2.1b	2.2b	2.3b	2.4b	2.5b	3.1b	3.2b	4.1b	4.2b	4.3b
	1.1c	1.2c	1.3c	2.1c	2.2c	2.3c		2.5c	3.1c		4.1c	4.2c	4.3c
	1.1d				2.2d				3.1d				4.3d
					2.2e								
					2.2f								
					2.2g								

ICT

ICT	ICT 1 finding out		ICT 2 ideas	ICT 3 reviewing	ICT 4 breadth
	1.1a	1.2a	2a	3a	4a
	1.1b	1.2b	2b	3b	4b
	1.1c	`1.2c	2c	3c	4c
		1.2d			

History

History	H1 chronology	H2 events, people	H3 interpret	H4 enquire	H5 org & comm	H6 breadth
	1a	2a	3a	4a	5a	6a
	1b	2b		4b		6b
						6c
						6d

Geography

Geography	G1.1 & G1.2 enquiry		G2 places	G3 processes	G4 environment	G5 breadth
	1.1a	1.2a	2a	3a	4a	5a
	1.1b	1.2b	2b	3b	4b	5b
	1.1c	1.2c	2c			5c
	1.1d	1.2d	2d			5d
			2e			

PE

PE	PE1 devel skills	PE2 apply skills	PE3 evaluate	PE4 fitness	PE5 breadth
	1a	2a	3a	4a	5a dance
	1b	2b	3b	4b	5b games
		2c	3c		5c gym

Art & Design

Art & Design	A&D1 ideas	A&D2 making	A&D3 evaluating	A&D4 materials	A&D5 breadth
	1a	2a	3a	4a	5a
	1b	2b	3b	4b	5b
		2c		4c	5c
					5d

PHSE & C

PHSE & C	PSHEC1 conf & resp	PSHEC2 citizenship	PSHEC3 health	PSHEC4 relationships
	1a	2a	3a	4a
	1b	2b	3b	4b
	1c	2c	3c	4c
	1d	2d	3d	4d
	1e	2e	3e	4e
		2f	3f	
		2g	3g	
		2h		

D&T

D&T	D&T 1 developing	D&T 2 tool use	D&T 3 evaluating	D&T 4 materials	D&T 5 breadth
	1a	2a	3a	4a	5a
	1b	2b	3b	4b	5b
	1c	2c			5c
	1d	2d			
	1e	2e			

Music

Music	M1 performing	M2 composing	M3 appraising	M4 listening	M5 breadth
	1a	2a	3a	4a	5a
	1b	2b	3b	4b	5b
	1c			4c	5c
					5d

Key to KS1 PoS on Pages 69-74

Critical Skills / Thinking Skills

Critical Skills	Thinking Skills
problem solving	observing
decision making	classifying
critical thinking	prediction
creative thinking	making inferences
communication	problem solving
organisation	drawing conclusions
management	
leadership	

Date	
Names	

Notes on how to take the learning forward:

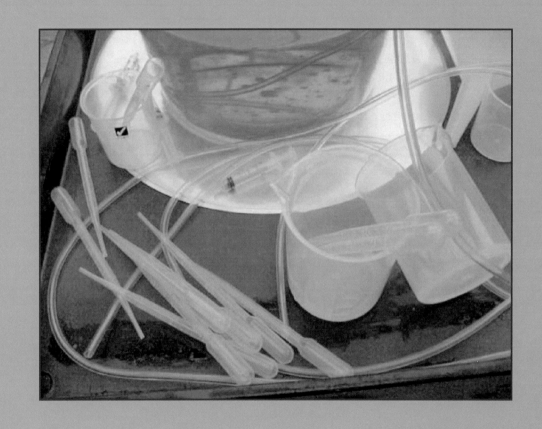

Droppers, syringes and pipettes

Droppers, syringes, pipettes

Previous experience in the Foundation Stage.
Children will have had experience of using droppers and pipettes in the Foundation Stage. They are familiar tools for:

* free play in water trays and boxes indoors and in the garden;
* filling and emptying small containers and bottles;
* dripping and dropping in creative activities with paint, dye and food colouring;
* collecting small amounts of water in corners and the bottom of containers;
* mixing and exploring coloured water and other liquids.

Pause for thought
In the early stages of working with these materials it is crucial to continue to observe the children. Only by doing this can you set developmentally appropriate challenges and provocations. The ideas listed here are offered as suggestions; the most exciting challenges will arise from children's own interests and motivations, which will only become apparent as you spend time with them, watching and joining them in their play. As you do this, you will be moving between the three interconnecting roles of observer, co-player, extender described below, and will be able to decide what you need to do next to take the learning forward.

The responsive adult (see page 5)
In three interconnecting roles, the responsive adult will be:

* observing
* listening
* interpreting

observer

* modelling
* playing alongside
* offering suggestions
* responding sensitively
* initiating with care!

co-player

* discussing ideas
* sharing thinking
* modelling new skills
* asking open questions
* being an informed extender
* instigating ideas & thoughts
* supporting children as they make links in learning
* making possibilities evident
* introducing new ideas and resources
* offering challenges and provocations

extender

Offering Challenges and Provocations - some ideas:
As children get older they can manage much smaller versions of the tools they have been using in the Foundation Stage. Plastic pipettes, tubing and syringes are very cheap from science supply catalogues of websites.

? Collect some very small containers and bottles. Look around at home and at school to see what you can find. Fill them with water - you may have to use a tiny funnel. Now use pipettes and syringes to get the water out of the containers.

? Use pipettes and some different colours of food colouring to colour containers of water. How many different shades and colours can you make? What happens if you mix the colours? can you make shades of the colours by using different amounts of colouring?

? How does a pipette work? look carefully and talk with a friend about this, and draw a diagram to show how they work. Do syringes work in the same way?

? Find some paper towels and use pipettes to explore how absorbent the towels are, and what happens to the water.

? Colour some water in different shades, and use pipettes and syringes to make patterns on paper, paper towels or tissues.

? Try writing your name or a word on a tissue, using a pipette. Is it easy?

? Paint a piece of strong paper or thin card with clear water. Now use the pipettes and runny paint or coloured water to make pictures on the paper. What happens?

? Fill a container with water. Now use a pipette to completely empty the the container without touching the water or the container.

? Find some plastic sheeting or a piece cut from a plastic carrier bag. Use the pipettes and syringes to explore how coloured water behaves when you drop it on plastic.

Ready for more?

- Fill a tall transparent container with clear water. Use droppers and pipettes to drop inks or undiluted food colouring into the water. Do it a drop at a time and watch what happens. Take some photos. Try adding another colour. What happens now?

- Work with friend to find a way to catch a drop of colouring underwater after it has been dropped. How easy is this to do?

- Use colourings to make a range of shades of one colour. Find a way to record the range of shades you make.

- Using just red, blue and yellow colourings, can you make these colours? Green, brown, pink, orange, purple, black, grey.

- Why do you think doctors use syringes to give injections to people and animals? See if you can find out from books and the internet.

- Use a syringe with a measure on the side to measure exact amounts of water. Why is it important to be able to measure the amount in the syringe? Why do doctors, dentists, vets, chefs, nurses and animal hunters need to measure carefully when they fill a syringe?

- Find some small transparent containers and fill them with dry or damp sand. Now use pipettes and syringes to explore what happens when you drop or inject water into the sand. Take some photos.

Materials, equipment, suppliers, websites, books and other references

Suppliers of cheap plastic science equipment:
For syringes, pipettes and tubing suitable for school use :
www.philipharris.co.uk
ASCO Educational; suppliers of equipment and tools for water play:
Other education suppliers will have more equipment, try;
Eduzone: www.eduzone.co.uk
TTS Group have a wide range of water tools and containers: www.tts-group.co.uk
Get plastic tubing from aquarium suppliers, garden centres and DIY shops.
Food colouring in big bottles from www.tts-group.co.uk

For images of water try **Google Images**. Just enter a word of something you want to see, and pictures will appear ('drop' 'waterfall' 'funnel' 'dropper' 'pipette' etc).
Fact sheets on water are available on www.bbc.co.uk/health or ga.water.usgs.gov - the US government education site for water with pictures and facts.
Look at www.liquidsculpture.com for some breathtaking images of water drops.

Some suitable **books** for younger readers include:
Sand and Water Play: Simple, Creative Activities for Young Children; Sherrie West; Gryphon House
The Little Book of Sand and Water; Sally Featherstone; Featherstone Education

Curriculum coverage grid overleaf

Potential NC KS1 Curriculum Coverage through the provocations suggested for droppers, syringes and pipettes

Literacy	Lit 1 speak	Lit 2 listen	Lit 3 group	Lit 4 drama	Lit 5 word	Lit 6 spell	Lit 7 text1	Lit 8 text2	Lit 9 text3	Lit10 text4	Lit11 sentence	Lit12 presentation
	1.1	2.1	3.1	4.1	5.1	6.1	7.1	8.1	9.1	10.1	11.1	12.1
	1.2	2.2	3.2	4.2	5.2	6.2	7.2	8.2	9.2	10.2	11.2	12.2

Numeracy	Num 1 U&A	Num 2 count	Num 3 number	Num 4 calculate	Num 5 shape	Num 6 measure	Num 7 data
	1.1	2.1	3.1	4.1	5.1	6.1	7.1
	1.2	2.2	3.2	4.2	5.2	6.2	7.2

Science	SC1 Enquiry			SC2 Life processes					SC3 Materials		SC4 Phys processes		
	Sc1.1	Sc1.2	Sc1.3	Sc2.1	Sc2.2	Sc2.3	Sc2.4	Sc2.5	Sc3.1	Sc3.2	Sc4.1	Sc4.2	Sc4.3
	1.1a	1.2a	1.3a	2.1a	2.2a	2.3a	2.4a	2.5a	3.1a	3.2a	4.1a	4.2a	4.3a
	1.1b	1.2b	1.3b	2.1b	2.2b	2.3b	2.4b	2.5b	3.1b	3.2b	4.1b	4.2b	4.3b
	1.1c	1.2c	1.3c	2.1c	2.2c	2.3c		2.5c	3.1c		4.1c	4.2c	4.3c
	1.1d				2.2d				3.1d				4.3d
					2.2e								
					2.2f								
					2.2g								

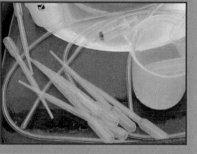

ICT	ICT 1 finding out		ICT 2 ideas	ICT 3 reviewing	ICT 4 breadth
	1.1a	1.2a	2a	3a	4a
	1.1b	1.2b	2b	3b	4b
	1.1c	1.2c	2c	3c	4c
		1.2d			

Full version of KS1 PoS on pages 69-74
Photocopiable version on page 8

History	H1 chronology	H2 events, people	H3 interpret	H4 enquire	H5 org & comm	H6 breadth
	1a	2a	3a	4a	5a	6a
	1b	2b		4b		6b
						6c
						6d

Geography	G1.1 & G1.2 enquiry		G2 places	G3 processes	G4 environment	G5 breadth
	1.1a	1.2a	2a	3a	4a	5a
	1.1b	1.2b	2b	3b	4b	5b
	1.1c	1.2c	2c			5c
	1.1d	1.2d	2d			5d
			2e			

D&T	D&T 1 developing	D&T 2 tool use	D&T 3 evaluating	D&T 4 materials	D&T 5 breadth
	1a	2a	3a	4a	5a
	1b	2b	3b	4b	5b
	1c	2c			5c
	1d	2d			
	1e	2e			

Music	M1 performing	M2 composing	M3 appraising	M4 listening	M5 breadth
	1a	2a	3a	4a	5a
	1b	2b	3b	4b	5b
	1c			4c	5c
					5d

PHSE & C	PSHEC1 conf & resp	PSHEC2 citizenship	PSHEC3 health	PSHEC4 relationships
	1a	2a	3a	4a
	1b	2b	3b	4b
	1c	2c	3c	4c
	1d	2d	3d	4d
	1e	2e	3e	4e
		2f	3f	
		2g	3g	
		2h		

Art & Design	A&D1 ideas	A&D2 making	A&D3 evaluating	A&D4 materials	A&D5 breadth
	1a	2a	3a	4a	5a
	1b	2b	3b	4b	5b
		2c		4c	5c
					5d

PE	PE1 devel skills	PE2 apply skills	PE3 evaluate	PE4 fitness	PE5 breadth
	1a	2a	3a	4a	5a dance
	1b	2b	3b	4b	5b games
		2c	3c		5c gym

Critical skills	Thinking Skills
problem solving	observing
decision making	classifying
critical thinking	prediction
creative thinking	making inferences
communication	problem solving
organisation	drawing conclusions
management	
leadership	

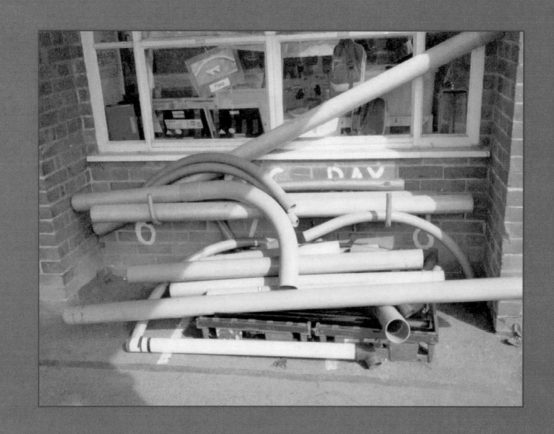

Guttering and drainpipes

Guttering & drainpipes

Previous experience in the Foundation Stage.
Guttering and drainpipes are now a feature of most early years settings, and the majority of children will have experimented with and explored these resources:
* in free play indoors and out of doors;
* in sand and water play;
* in focused work on weather and rainfall;
* in recreating stories and rhymes such as Incey Wincey Spider;
* in imaginative play where pipes and guttering may have been used to represent a variety of objects in scenes, shelters and structures;
* in experimentation, making slopes, tunnels, roadways, for moving balls, cars, sand, gravel, rice, water etc.

Pause for thought
In the early stages of working with these materials it is crucial to continue to observe the children. Only by doing this can you set developmentally appropriate challenges and provocations. The ideas listed here are offered as suggestions; the most exciting challenges will arise from children's own interests and motivations, which will only become apparent as you spend time with them, watching and joining them in their play. As you do this, you will be moving between the three interconnecting roles of observer, co-player, extender described below, and will be able to decide what you need to do next to take the learning forward.

The responsive adult (see page 5)

In three interconnecting roles, the responsive adult will be:

observer
* observing
* listening
* interpreting

co-player
* **modelling**
* **playing alongside**
* **offering suggestions**
* **responding sensitively**
* **initiating with care!**

extender
* discussing ideas
* sharing thinking
* modelling new skills
* asking open questions
* being an informed extender
* instigating ideas & thoughts
* supporting children as they make links in learning
* making possibilities evident
* introducing new ideas and resources
* offering challenges and provocations

Offering Challenges and Provocations - some ideas:

? Can you make a waterway for small boats?
? Make a waterway with guttering and then use stones, pebbles, sticks, twigs and sand to make a dam.
? Can you build a waterway with two, three, four or five bends or corners?
? Can you invent a way of collecting rainwater using your pipes and guttering? Collect water in different places and measure how much you collect in each place. Which place is best?
? Make a waterfall with guttering - how high can you make it? What can you use to collect the water at the bottom of the waterfall?
? Have a regatta or boat race, using your guttering as a river. Work with your friends to set up the course, choose a small boat each and see how you can make your boat win a race.
? Can you make some boats with sails, and sail them on the river you have made? You could use polystyrene trays, plastic plates or other recycled materials. What is the best way to make the boats move along the guttering and through the pipes?
? Try pouring coloured water down guttering into a bowl of clear water. Watch carefully what happens.
? Can you find ways to join the pipes together so they don't leak? What works best? Try
   • duct tape
   • gaffer tape
   • sellotape
   • brown parcel tape
   • masking tape
Can you make a chart or graph to show the results of your experiments?

Ready for more?

- Use the guttering to make rivers in a small world landscape. Add grass, paths, trees and other objects on the banks of the rivers and streams.
- Find out how to play 'Pooh Sticks'. Make a game for yourselves, where you can race small sticks or leaves along a guttering racetrack. How can you make them go faster or slow down?
- Google 'waterfalls' and 'white water'. Can you add stones and boulders to your waterway to make white water and rapids?
- Use piping in sand to make an underground river or tunnel.
- Use the internet and books to research different sorts of water features. Can you create a water feature with the guttering and pipes?
- Find a clipboard and go round your school to locate all the guttering and piping you can find. Watch these when it rains and see how they work and if any of them are blocked. Could you invent a tool to unblock drainpipes or guttering?
- Find some empty plastic water bottles, make holes in them, and fix them to plastic tubing to make showers or sprinklers.
- What is the longest waterway you can make? Can you make a waterway on several levels? Look on the internet for pictures of canals and aqueducts.

Materials, equipment, suppliers, websites, books and other references

Suppliers of plastic piping and other rainwater supplies:

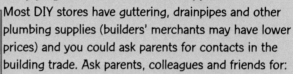

Most DIY stores have guttering, drainpipes and other plumbing supplies (builders' merchants may have lower prices) and you could ask parents for contacts in the building trade. Ask parents, colleagues and friends for:

- old CLEAN guttering and drainpipes
- hose from washing machines, tumble driers and vacuum cleaners

Builders' trays (or cement mixing trays) are very useful for containing the water during experiments. Get these from DIY superstores such as B&Q, Wilkinson's or Homebase.

TTS Group www.tts-group.co.uk or www.philipharris.co.uk have a wide range of equipment. Get cat litter trays or washing up bowls from a bargain shop for space saving water play.

www.plumbworld.co.uk has an incredible variety of branded water pipes, at Internet-only prices, and www.screwfix.com has a vast range of plumbing equipment to look at.

For useful images of water and the water cycle, weather and natural features of rain, try **Google Images**. Just enter the name of what you want to see ('plumber' 'water cycle' 'drain' 'aqueduct' 'monsoon' etc) for hundreds of images of different sorts.

www.wateraid.org/uk is a site for charity collections to support water aid.

www.kidzone.ws/water has fun facts for kids about the Water Cycle, including photos, activity suggestions and some printable worksheets.

Some suitable books for younger readers include:

The Biography of Splash the Raindrop; Gary Piper; Publish America
The Little Raindrop; Wendy Garrison; Findhorn Press
The Adventures of Robbie the Raindrop; John Carroll; Tate Publishing
Down the Drain; Richard Powell; Tiger Tales
Down the Drain; Conserving Water; Anita Ganeri; Heinemann
Ants in the Drain; Uncle Fez; Trafford Publishing
Earthwise, Water; Jim Pipe; Franklin Watts
Mrs Plug The Plumber; Allan Ahlberg: Puffin
Plumber; Katherine Frew; Children's Press
A Day with the Plumber: Mark Thomas; Children's Press

Curriculum coverage grid overleaf

Potential NC KS1 Curriculum Coverage through the provocations suggested for guttering and drainpipes.

Full version of KS1 PoS on pages 69-74
Photocopiable version on page 8

Literacy

Lit 1 speak	Lit 2 listen	Lit 3 group	Lit 4 drama	Lit 5 word	Lit 6 spell	Lit 7 text1	Lit 8 text2	Lit 9 text3	Lit10 text4	Lit11 sentence	Lit12 presentation
1.1	2.1	3.1	4.1	5.1	6.1	7.1	8.1	9.1	10.1	11.1	12.1
1.2	2.2	3.2	4.2	5.2	6.2	7.2	8.2	9.2	10.2	11.2	12.2

Numeracy

Num 1 U&A	Num 2 count	Num 3 number	Num 4 calculate	Num 5 shape	Num 6 measure	Num 7 data
1.1	2.1	3.1	4.1	5.1	6.1	7.1
1.2	2.2	3.2	4.2	5.2	6.2	7.2

Science

SC1 Enquiry			SC2 Life processes					SC3 Materials		SC4 Phys processes		
Sc1.1	Sc1.2	Sc1.3	Sc2.1	Sc2.2	Sc2.3	Sc2.4	Sc2.5	Sc3.1	Sc3.2	Sc4.1	Sc4.2	Sc4.3
1.1a	1.2a	1.3a	2.1a	2.2a	2.3a	2.4a	2.5a	3.1a	3.2a	4.1a	4.2a	4.3a
1.1b	1.2b	1.3b	2.1b	2.2b	2.3b	2.4b	2.5b	3.1b	3.2b	4.1b	4.2b	4.3b
1.1c	1.2c	1.3c	2.1c	2.2c	2.3c		2.5c	3.1c		4.1c	4.2c	4.3c
1.1d				2.2d				3.1d				4.3d
				2.2e								
				2.2f								
				2.2g								

ICT

ICT 1 finding out		ICT 2 ideas	ICT 3 reviewing	ICT 4 breadth
1.1a	1.2a	2a	3a	4a
1.1b	1.2b	2b	3b	4b
1.1c	1.2c	2c	3c	4c
	1.2d			

D&T

D&T 1 developing	D&T 2 tool use	D&T 3 evaluating	D&T 4 materials	D&T 5 breadth
1a	2a	3a	4a	5a
1b	2b	3b	4b	5b
1c	2c			5c
1d	2d			
1e	2e			

History

H1 chronology	H2 events, people	H3 interpret	H4 enquire	H5 org & comm	H6 breadth
1a	2a	3a	4a	5a	6a
1b	2b		4b		6b
					6c
					6d

Geography

G1.1 & G1.2 enquiry		G2 places	G3 processes	G4 environment	G5 breadth
1.1a	1.2a	2a	3a	4a	5a
1.1b	1.2b	2b	3b	4b	5b
1.1c	1.2c	2c			5c
1.1d	1.2d	2d			5d
		2e			

Music

M1 performing	M2 composing	M3 appraising	M4 listening	M5 breadth
1a	2a	3a	4a	5a
1b	2b	3b	4b	5b
1c			4c	5c
				5d

PHSE & C

PSHEC1 conf & resp	PSHEC2 citizenship	PSHEC3 health	PSHEC4 relationships
1a	2a	3a	4a
1b	2b	3b	4b
1c	2c	3c	4c
1d	2d	3d	4d
1e	2e	3e	4e
	2f	3f	
	2g	3g	
	2h		

Art & Design

A&D1 ideas	A&D2 making	A&D3 evaluating	A&D4 materials	A&D5 breadth
1a	2a	3a	4a	5a
1b	2b	3b	4b	5b
	2c		4c	5c
				5d

PE

PE1 devel skills	PE2 apply skills	PE3 evaluate	PE4 fitness	PE5 breadth
1a	2a	3a	4a	5a dance
1b	2b	3b	4b	5b games
	2c	3c		5c gym

Critical skills	Thinking Skills
problem solving	observing
decision making	classifying
critical thinking	prediction
creative thinking	making inferences
communication	problem solving
organisation	drawing conclusions
management	
leadership	

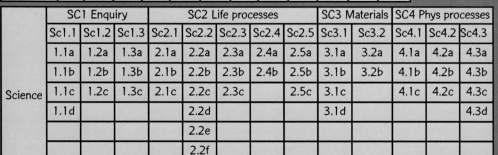

Syphoning

Syphoning

Previous experience in the Foundation Stage.

By the time children leave the Foundation Stage they should have had some experience of using simple syphons in water play:

* in free play indoors and out of doors;
* in role play situations;
* in play with guttering and drainpipes;
* to explore ways of moving water from one level to another;
* when playing with buckets, tubing and other simple science equipment.

They should also have had experience of:

* talking about how water moves, and how gravity affects this movement;
* using their skills and creativity to make water do what they want.

Pause for thought

In the early stages of working with these materials it is crucial to continue to observe the children. Only by doing this can you set developmentally appropriate challenges and provocations. The ideas listed here are offered as suggestions; the most exciting challenges will arise from children's own interests and motivations, which will only become apparent as you spend time with them, watching and joining them in their play. As you do this, you will be moving between the three interconnecting roles of observer, co-player, extender described below, and will be able to decide what you need to do next to take the learning forward.

The responsive adult (see page 5)

In three interconnecting roles, the responsive adult will be:

* observing
* listening
* interpreting

observer

* **modelling**
* **playing alongside**
* **offering suggestions**
* **responding sensitively**
* **initiating with care!**

co-player

* discussing ideas
* sharing thinking
* modelling new skills
* asking open questions
* being an informed extender
* instigating ideas & thoughts
* supporting children as they make links in learning
* making possibilities evident
* introducing new ideas and resources
* offering challenges and provocations

extender

Offering Challenges and Provocations - some ideas:

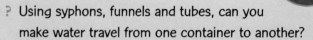

Children may need practice in accepting and carrying out challenges presented by adults, when they have been used to free play in water. You may need to introduce this gradually and sit with the children as they work to encourage them to stay on task!

? Using syphons, funnels and tubes, can you make water travel from one container to another?

? Put a bucket of water on a table, and an empty bucket on the floor. How can you get the water from the top bucket into the bottom bucket without moving either of the buckets?

? Can you use syphons and other water equipment to make a water feature in your playground? Draw some pictures before you start and take some photos of your finished work.

? Can you use syphons for other substances? Try them with sand, paint, flour, paste. Does a syphon work with all of these? Do you know why?

? Join a syphon to the end of a piece of tubing. Experiment with moving water along the tubing using the syphon. Try with the tubing flat, sloping down and sloping up.

? Can you fix up a series of syphons to move water between two or more containers such as plastic buckets.

? Collect or make some cylinders of different materials - card, rigid plastic, flexible plastic, bubble wrap. Can you use these to make syphons?

? Collect some empty pumps from hand soap or lotions. Use these to find out how hand pumps work. Are they the same as syphons?

Ready for more?

- Use the internet to find out how pumps are used in industry. Put 'hand pump' in Google Images and look for some pictures. Then click on some of the pictures and find out more about the websites behind the pictures.

- Look up 'fire engine pump' on Google Images.

- Then try people.howstuffworks.com and search for 'fire engine pump' to find some information and pictures of how fire engines work. You could also look at 'pump' on the same site for information on how washing machine pumps work.

- Find some empty hand pumps from soap or hand cream. Use these to make a machine that pumps water from one place to another. You could add plastic tubing and other containers. If you colour the water, it will be easier to see where it is going.

- Get a hand-held water spray (the sort for spraying indoor plants). Find out how it works, then think of six different ways to use the spray. It would be better to do this outside! At least one of the uses of the spray must be artistic.

- Search the internet, magazines, your school and home to see how many pumps, syphons and sprayers you can find. Don't forget to look under the sink!

Materials, equipment, suppliers, websites, books and other references

Syphons, plastic tubing and other useful containers from www.philipharris.co.uk www.tts-group.co.uk or **educational suppliers**.

ASCO www.ascoeducational.co.uk have a water play activity workshop and some great aqueduct sets for building big water constructions out of doors.

Get plastic pipettes cheap from www.esupply.co.uk - in packs of 100. There is a huge variety and range of types in suppliers catalogues and on their websites. Many suppliers have 'own brand' versions of water equipment, which are often cheaper, but may not be as durable. As with all educational equipment, you will get what you pay for - buy the best you can afford. For simple water containers such as buckets, bowls, plastic boxes etc. you can go to bargain shops or DIY stores. Pumps from hand soap and other cosmetics are another free resource, and you could try (clean) plant spray pumps, bike pumps and balloon pumps to explore the principles of syphons and pumping. Fire Stations and Fire Service sites will have information on fire engine pumps.

Look on www-saps.plantsci.cam.ac for information on self watering plants and worksheets lined to the KS1 curriculum, and at www.woodlands-junior.kent.sch.uk a school site with activities and worksheets. www.primaryschoolscience.com/clipart has good clipart of science equipment such as beakers for displays etc - look in the Chemistry section.

Some sites with pumping and hose equipment - www.flexiblehose.co.uk www.holmeshose.co.uk www.aflex-hose.co.uk www.hoseint.co.uk (drilling platforms).

Some suitable **books** for younger readers include:

Starting Point Science; Susan Mayes; Usborne
How it Works; neil Ardley; Readers Digest
Fire Engines;(Machines and Work); DK
Tonka; If I Could Drive a Fire Truck; Michael Teitelbaum; Cartwheel
Oil and Gas; John Zronik; Crabtree
From Oil to Gas; Shannon Zemlicka; Lerner
Oil and Gas; Neil Morris; Smart Apple Media
Rain Gardens; Nigel Dunnett; Timber Press

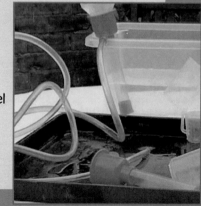

Curriculum coverage grid overleaf

Potential NC KS1 Curriculum Coverage through the provocations suggested for syphoning.

Full version of KS1 PoS on pages 69-74
Photocopiable version on page 8

Literacy

	Lit 1 speak	Lit 2 listen	Lit 3 group	Lit 4 drama	Lit 5 word	Lit 6 spell	Lit 7 text1	Lit 8 text2	Lit 9 text3	Lit10 text4	Lit11 sentence	Lit12 presentation
Literacy	1.1	2.1	3.1	4.1	5.1	6.1	7.1	8.1	9.1	10.1	11.1	12.1
	1.2	2.2	3.2	4.2	5.2	6.2	7.2	8.2	9.2	10.2	11.2	12.2

Numeracy

	Num 1 U&A	Num 2 count	Num 3 number	Num 4 calculate	Num 5 shape	Num 6 measure	Num 7 data
Numeracy	1.1	2.1	3.1	4.1	5.1	6.1	7.1
	1.2	2.2	3.2	4.2	5.2	6.2	7.2

Science

	SC1 Enquiry			SC2 Life processes					SC3 Materials		SC4 Phys processes		
	Sc1.1	Sc1.2	Sc1.3	Sc2.1	Sc2.2	Sc2.3	Sc2.4	Sc2.5	Sc3.1	Sc3.2	Sc4.1	Sc4.2	Sc4.3
Science	1.1a	1.2a	1.3a	2.1a	2.2a	2.3a	2.4a	2.5a	3.1a	3.2a	4.1a	4.2a	4.3a
	1.1b	1.2b	1.3b	2.1b	2.2b	2.3b	2.4b	2.5b	3.1b	3.2b	4.1b	4.2b	4.3b
	1.1c	1.2c	1.3c	2.1c	2.2c	2.3c		2.5c	3.1c		4.1c	4.2c	4.3c
	1.1d				2.2d				3.1d				4.3d
					2.2e								
					2.2f								
					2.2g								

ICT

	ICT 1 finding out	ICT 2 ideas	ICT 3 reviewing	ICT 4 breadth
ICT	1.1a / 1.2a	2a	3a	4a
	1.1b / 1.2b	2b	3b	4b
	1.1c / 1.2c	2c	3c	4c
	1.2d			

D&T

	D&T 1 developing	D&T 2 tool use	D&T 3 evaluating	D&T 4 materials	D&T 5 breadth
D&T	1a	2a	3a	4a	5a
	1b	2b	3b	4b	5b
	1c	2c			5c
	1d	2d			
	1e	2e			

History

	H1 chronology	H2 events, people	H3 interpret	H4 enquire	H5 org & comm	H6 breadth
History	1a	2a	3a	4a	5a	6a
	1b	2b		4b		6b
						6c
						6d

Geography

	G1.1 & G1.2 enquiry		G2 places	G3 processes	G4 environment	G5 breadth
Geography	1.1a	1.2a	2a	3a	4a	5a
	1.1b	1.2b	2b	3b	4b	5b
	1.1c	1.2c	2c			5c
	1.1d	1.2d	2d			5d
			2e			

Music

	M1 performing	M2 composing	M3 appraising	M4 listening	M5 breadth
Music	1a	2a	3a	4a	5a
	1b	2b	3b	4b	5b
	1c			4c	5c
					5d

PHSE & C

	PSHEC1 conf & resp	PSHEC2 citizenship	PSHEC3 health	PSHEC4 relationships
PHSE & C	1a	2a	3a	4a
	1b	2b	3b	4b
	1c	2c	3c	4c
	1d	2d	3d	4d
	1e	2e	3e	4e
		2f	3f	
		2g	3g	
		2h		

Art & Design

	A&D1 ideas	A&D2 making	A&D3 evaluating	A&D4 materials	A&D5 breadth
Art & Design	1a	2a	3a	4a	5a
	1b	2b	3b	4b	5b
		2c		4c	5c
					5d

PE

	PE1 devel skills	PE2 apply skills	PE3 evaluate	PE4 fitness	PE5 breadth
PE	1a	2a	3a	4a	5a dance
	1b	2b	3b	4b	5b games
		2c	3c		5c gym

Critical skills / Thinking Skills

Critical skills	Thinking Skills
problem solving	observing
decision making	classifying
critical thinking	prediction
creative thinking	making inferences
communication	problem solving
organisation	drawing conclusions
management	
leadership	

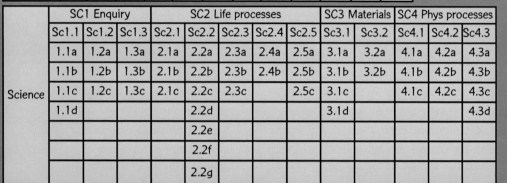

Moving water and water wheels

Water wheels

Previous experience in the Foundation Stage.

During their time in the Early Years Foundation Stage, children will have played in water trays with pipes, pumps, water wheels and pipettes:

* in free play indoors and out of doors.

They will have used these materials in exploratory and imaginative play and will have begun to explore their potential for moving water from one place to another.

* filling and emptying containers;
* spraying and squirting;
* lifting water with the wheels;
* using the wheels with bubbly and coloured water.

Pause for thought

In the early stages of working with these materials it is crucial to continue to observe the children. Only by doing this can you set developmentally appropriate challenges and provocations. The ideas listed here are offered as suggestions; the most exciting challenges will arise from children's own interests and motivations, which will only become apparent as you spend time with them, watching and joining them in their play. As you do this, you will be moving between the three interconnecting roles of observer, co-player, extender described below, and will be able to decide what you need to do next to take the learning forward.

The responsive adult (see page 5)

In three interconnecting roles, the responsive adult will be:

observer

* observing
* listening
* interpreting

co-player

* modelling
* playing alongside
* offering suggestions
* responding sensitively
* initiating with care!

extender

* discussing ideas
* sharing thinking
* modelling new skills
* asking open questions
* being an informed extender
* instigating ideas & thoughts
* supporting children as they make links in learning
* making possibilities evident
* introducing new ideas and resources
* offering challenges and provocations

Offering Challenges and Provocations - some ideas:

The challenge for KS1 teachers lies in providing provocations that allow children to draw on their previous experience and extend their knowledge in new and exciting ways.

? Measure a litre of water and then pour it through a water wheel into another container. Can you do this without losing any water? Measure the water at the end and see how much has been lost. Can you find out the how much has gone?

? How many ways can you find of moving water from one container to another? Try these:
  * syphoning
  * using a ladle or a spoon
  * with a pipette
  * making hole in the bottom of a container
  * using a funnel and tubing.

Which one works best?
Which is quickest?
Which wastes least water?

? Can you construct a water-run using:
  * one water wheel
  * two water wheels
  * three water wheels.

Measure the run - what is the longest you can make?

? Use the internet to find out how water wheels were made and how they worked. Do we still use water wheels now? Where?

? Google 'cascade'. Can you use construction pieces and other materials to make a water cascade? Photograph it.

? Can you use ropes and pulleys to lift water out of doors? Try using a climbing frame or fence to carry the weight.

? Fill a small bucket with water and move it three metres without losing any water. How did you do it? How did you check that you didn't lose any water?

Ready for more?

- Make a collection of washing up liquid bottles. Now find a way of testing them to see which one will squirt water furthest. Can you use the force from the bottles to move objects along the ground?

- Can you use some plastic cups to make a cascade? Find ways of fixing them so they work. Take some photos f your inventions.

- Fill a collection of plant misters or plant sprays with different colored water. Use these to make patterns and designs on different sorts of surfaces. Which surface works best?

- Make a landscape in a shallow tray, using sand, earth or clay. Can you move water round this landscape

- Try making your own water wheels from plastic, card, old wheels from pushchairs or trikes. You will need to find a way to fix the wheel in a vertical position, so it will turn round, then you can fix water containers onto the wheel.

- Can you make a Water Play World for Lego or Playmobil people? You could make a water chute, log flume, water slide or helter skelter.

- Add some guttering and drainpipes to your water wheels and make water move further and further. Float objects down the moving water.

Materials, equipment, suppliers, websites, books and other references

Making water move has a constant fascination for all humans. Children will use water wheels, guttering and drainpipes to do this, and you may want to add some specialist equipment to make it even more fun:

TTS www.tts-group.co.uk and ASCO www.ascoeducational.co.uk have water viaduct sets as well as water wheels and other simple water equipment.

For inspiration, try putting some words in Google - 'water wheel' 'water sculpture' 'fountain' 'waterfall' 'water park' 'water chute' 'water feature' www.waterwheelfactory.com or www.leahy-hill.com will take you to working water mills and a water wheel factory. www.reuk.co.uk has an explanation of how water wheels work (click through to 'hydro').

www.williampye.com is a great site for water sculpture - click on 'sources of information' and the 'large and small works' sections to see 'Brimming Bowl', 'Scylla' and 'Archimedes' water sculptures.

Some **book** titles:
Pools; Kelly Kline: Rizzoli (architectural coffee table book)
The Water Gardener; John Brookes; Frances Lincoln
Ponds and Lakes; Spotter's Guide; Usborne
Hamish McHaggis: The Wonderful Water Wheel (Hamish McHaggis) by Linda Strachan and Sally J. Collins; GW Publishing
The Fish and the Water Wheel; Christopher Pilkington; Patmos
Roberto and the Magic Fountain; Donna Vann; Lion Hudson
Little Eagle and the Sacred Waterfall; (Native American Tale); Howard Losness; Universe
The Wonder of a Waterfall; Allan Fowler; Children's Press
The Highest Waterfall; Stuart Kallen; Kidhaven Press

Curriculum coverage grid overleaf

Potential NC KS1 Curriculum Coverage through the provocations suggested for moving water.

Literacy	Lit 1 speak	Lit 2 listen	Lit 3 group	Lit 4 drama	Lit 5 word	Lit 6 spell	Lit 7 text1	Lit 8 text2	Lit 9 text3	Lit10 text4	Lit11 sentence	Lit12 presentation
	1.1	2.1	3.1	4.1	5.1	6.1	7.1	8.1	9.1	10.1	11.1	12.1
	1.2	2.2	3.2	4.2	5.2	6.2	7.2	8.2	9.2	10.2	11.2	12.2

Numeracy	Num 1 U&A	Num 2 count	Num 3 number	Num 4 calculate	Num 5 shape	Num 6 measure	Num 7 data
	1.1	2.1	3.1	4.1	5.1	6.1	7.1
	1.2	2.2	3.2	4.2	5.2	6.2	7.2

Full version of KS1 PoS on pages 69-74
Photocopiable version on page 8

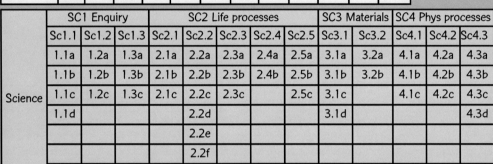

Science

	SC1 Enquiry			SC2 Life processes					SC3 Materials		SC4 Phys processes		
	Sc1.1	Sc1.2	Sc1.3	Sc2.1	Sc2.2	Sc2.3	Sc2.4	Sc2.5	Sc3.1	Sc3.2	Sc4.1	Sc4.2	Sc4.3
	1.1a	1.2a	1.3a	2.1a	2.2a	2.3a	2.4a	2.5a	3.1a	3.2a	4.1a	4.2a	4.3a
	1.1b	1.2b	1.3b	2.1b	2.2b	2.3b	2.4b	2.5b	3.1b	3.2b	4.1b	4.2b	4.3b
	1.1c	1.2c	1.3c	2.1c	2.2c	2.3c		2.5c	3.1c		4.1c	4.2c	4.3c
	1.1d				2.2d				3.1d				4.3d
					2.2e								
					2.2f								
					2.2g								

ICT

ICT	ICT 1 finding out		ICT 2 ideas	ICT 3 reviewing	ICT 4 breadth
	1.1a	1.2a	2a	3a	4a
	1.1b	1.2b	2b	3b	4b
	1.1c	1.2c	2c	3c	4c
		1.2d			

History

History	H1 chronology	H2 events, people	H3 interpret	H4 enquire	H5 org & comm	H6 breadth
	1a	2a	3a	4a	5a	6a
	1b	2b		4b		6b
						6c
						6d

Geography

Geography	G1.1 & G1.2 enquiry		G2 places	G3 processes	G4 environment	G5 breadth
	1.1a	1.2a	2a	3a	4a	5a
	1.1b	1.2b	2b	3b	4b	5b
	1.1c	1.2c	2c			5c
	1.1d	1.2d	2d			5d
			2e			

D&T

D&T	D&T 1 developing	D&T 2 tool use	D&T 3 evaluating	D&T 4 materials	D&T 5 breadth
	1a	2a	3a	4a	5a
	1b	2b	3b	4b	5b
	1c	2c			5c
	1d	2d			
	1e	2e			

Music

Music	M1 performing	M2 composing	M3 appraising	M4 listening	M5 breadth
	1a	2a	3a	4a	5a
	1b	2b	3b	4b	5b
	1c			4c	5c
					5d

PHSE & C

PHSE & C	PSHEC1 conf & resp	PSHEC2 citizenship	PSHEC3 health	PSHEC4 relationships
	1a	2a	3a	4a
	1b	2b	3b	4b
	1c	2c	3c	4c
	1d	2d	3d	4d
	1e	2e	3e	4e
		2f	3f	
		2g	3g	
		2h		

Art & Design

Art & Design	A&D1 ideas	A&D2 making	A&D3 evaluating	A&D4 materials	A&D5 breadth
	1a	2a	3a	4a	5a
	1b	2b	3b	4b	5b
		2c		4c	5c
					5d

PE

PE	PE1 devel skills	PE2 apply skills	PE3 evaluate	PE4 fitness	PE5 breadth
	1a	2a	3a	4a	5a dance
	1b	2b	3b	4b	5b games
		2c	3c		5c gym

Critical skills	Thinking Skills
problem solving	observing
decision making	classifying
critical thinking	prediction
creative thinking	making inferences
communication	problem solving
organisation	drawing conclusions
management	
leadership	

Boats and harbours

Boats and harbours

Previous experience in the Foundation Stage.
Small world boats are a favourite part of water play in the Early Years Foundation Stage and at home. Most children will have already spent time exploring:

* aspects of floating and sinking;
* boats as part of free play indoors and outside;
* making boats, leaves and other objects float in puddles and ponds;
* seeing, sailing and riding in boats in parks and at the seaside.

Pause for thought

In the early stages of working with these materials it is crucial to continue to observe the children. Only by doing this can you set developmentally appropriate challenges and provocations. The ideas listed here are offered as suggestions; the most exciting challenges will arise from children's own interests and motivations, which will only become apparent as you spend time with them, watching and joining them in their play. As you do this, you will be moving between the three interconnecting roles of observer, co-player, extender described below, and will be able to decide what you need to do next to take the learning forward.

The responsive adult (see page 5)

In three interconnecting roles, the responsive adult will be:

observer

* observing
* listening
* interpreting

co-player

* **modelling**
* **playing alongside**
* **offering suggestions**
* **responding sensitively**
* **initiating with care!**

extender

* discussing ideas
* sharing thinking
* modelling new skills
* asking open questions
* being an informed extender
* instigating ideas & thoughts
* supporting children as they make links in learning
* making possibilities evident
* introducing new ideas and resources
* offering challenges and provocations

Offering Challenges and Provocations - some ideas:

? Look for some small plastic boats. Test each one to see how much it will carry before it sinks. Try small stones, lego bricks, plastic animals, spoonfuls of sand, Play People.

? Try the test again in water with waves. How can you make some waves? What happens to the boats in the miniature storm?

? Create a small world for your boats. You could make a harbour, a fishing village, or an island. Use books and the internet to help you do this. Use Google Images for pictures of 'fishing boat' 'island' 'catamaran' 'harbour'.

? Google 'coracle' and find out what it is. Try designing and making one.

? Use recycled materials such as plastic bottles and pots, wood, plasticene, foil dishes etc. to make some boats. Test your boats in water. Which materials work best? Photograph some of your best work.

? How can you make your boat waterproof? What could you use? You could try some of these - PVA glue, plastic, cling film, polythene, paint, foil. Which works best?

? Put 'sailing ships' in Google Images. Can you make a boat with sails?

? Put 'narrow boat' or 'canal barge' in Google Images. Can you design and make your own narrow boat? How much weight will it carry?

? Google 'Vikings' or 'Norvik'. Can you work with some friends to make a Viking ship?

? Make a boating lake or harbour in some big containers such as plastic bowls, plant pots or ice cream tubs. Find out what you need to make by looking in books or on the internet. Get some friends to help you and take your time so the boating lake is the best you can make it.

Ready for more?

- Can you design a boat that will carry passengers? Start by making a boat that will carry two passengers, then gradually increase your challenge to four, then six, then more.

- Choose a soft toy or a bag of small objects such as marbles or Lego bricks. Now design and make a boat that will carry your load.

- Make a pirate ship, then make an island for it to sail to. You could make a treasure map and put some characters on your ship. Make a story up with your friends and tell it as you take some photos or video. Invite your friends to a film show of your pirate story.

- Use a big piece of board or card and stick a bin liner filled with screwed upnewspaper in the middle to make an island for boats to sail round. Can you make an island in the middle of some water?

- Use the Internet to find out all you can about making boats. Now make a powerpoint presentation or a photo information book with instructions for making toy boats. Illustrate your book with photos and diagrams.

- Get a copy of a story called Treasure Island by Robert Louis Stevenson. Read it yourself or ask someone to read it to you. Make your own book about Treasure Island, with maps, pictures and words.

Materials, equipment suppliers, websites, books and other references

Collect all sorts of model boats from bargain toy shops or from educational suppliers. It's also useful to have plenty of plastic containers and other recycled materials for making boats and harbours. Offer different sorts of tape and glues, but make sure there is plenty of waterproof tape (duct tape or similar) to avoid disappointment when they get wet.

Try some 'big ship' websites such as www.hms-victory.com - the official website for HMS Victory, www.titanic-titanic.com, www.historyonthenet.com or www.jorvik-viking-centre.co.uk for Vikings and their ships. Or try www.cunard.co.uk and order a cruise brochure.

For images of boats and ships, try **Google Images**, 'titanic' 'ocean liner' 'hms victory' 'fishing boat' 'power boat' 'sailing boat'.

Some suitable **books for younger readers** include:

Inside the Titanic; Ken Marschall; Little,Brown
Ships, Look inside Cross sections: Moir Butterfield; DK
The Story of Ships; Jane Bingham; Usborne
Stephen Biesty's Cross Sections; Stephen Biesty; DK
Titanic; Anna Claybourne; Usborne
Water and Boats; Jon Richards; Franklin Watts
Boats; Ian Rohr; A&C Black
Brilliant Boats; Tony Mitton; Kingfisher Books
The Little Boat; Kathy Henderson; Walker Books
The Goodbye Boat; Mary Joslin; Lion Hudson
All Afloat on Noah's Boat; Tony Mitton; Orchard Books
The Boat; Helen Ward; Simply Read
Ebb and Flo and the New Friend; Jane Simmons; Aladdin
The Green Ship; Quentin Blake; Red Fox
The Sea Monster; Christopher Wormell; Red Fox

Curriculum coverage grid overleaf

Potential NC KS1 Curriculum Coverage through the provocations suggested for boats and harbours.

Full version of KS1 PoS on pages 69-74
Photocopiable version on page 8

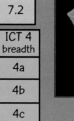

Literacy

	Lit 1 speak	Lit 2 listen	Lit 3 group	Lit 4 drama	Lit 5 word	Lit 6 spell	Lit 7 text1	Lit 8 text2	Lit 9 text3	Lit10 text4	Lit11 sentence	Lit12 presentation
	1.1	2.1	3.1	4.1	5.1	6.1	7.1	8.1	9.1	10.1	11.1	12.1
	1.2	2.2	3.2	4.2	5.2	6.2	7.2	8.2	9.2	10.2	11.2	12.2

Numeracy

	Num 1 U&A	Num 2 count	Num 3 number	Num 4 calculate	Num 5 shape	Num 6 measure	Num 7 data
	1.1	2.1	3.1	4.1	5.1	6.1	7.1
	1.2	2.2	3.2	4.2	5.2	6.2	7.2

Science

	SC1 Enquiry			SC2 Life processes					SC3 Materials		SC4 Phys processes		
	Sc1.1	Sc1.2	Sc1.3	Sc2.1	Sc2.2	Sc2.3	Sc2.4	Sc2.5	Sc3.1	Sc3.2	Sc4.1	Sc4.2	Sc4.3
	1.1a	1.2a	1.3a	2.1a	2.2a	2.3a	2.4a	2.5a	3.1a	3.2a	4.1a	4.2a	4.3a
	1.1b	1.2b	1.3b	2.1b	2.2b	2.3b	2.4b	2.5b	3.1b	3.2b	4.1b	4.2b	4.3b
	1.1c	1.2c	1.3c	2.1c	2.2c	2.3c		2.5c	3.1c		4.1c	4.2c	4.3c
	1.1d				2.2d				3.1d				4.3d
					2.2e								
					2.2f								
					2.2g								

ICT

	ICT 1 finding out	ICT 2 ideas	ICT 3 reviewing	ICT 4 breadth
	1.1a 1.2a	2a	3a	4a
	1.1b 1.2b	2b	3b	4b
	1.1c 1.2c	2c	3c	4c
	1.2d			

D&T

	D&T 1 developing	D&T 2 tool use	D&T 3 evaluating	D&T 4 materials	D&T 5 breadth
	1a	2a	3a	4a	5a
	1b	2b	3b	4b	5b
	1c	2c			5c
	1d	2d			
	1e	2e			

History

	H1 chronology	H2 events, people	H3 interpret	H4 enquire	H5 org & comm	H6 breadth
	1a	2a	3a	4a	5a	6a
	1b	2b		4b		6b
						6c
						6d

Geography

	G1.1 & G1.2 enquiry	G2 places	G3 processes	G4 environment	G5 breadth
	1.1a 1.2a	2a	3a	4a	5a
	1.1b 1.2b	2b	3b	4b	5b
	1.1c 1.2c	2c			5c
	1.1d 1.2d	2d			5d
		2e			

Music

	M1 performing	M2 composing	M3 appraising	M4 listening	M5 breadth
	1a	2a	3a	4a	5a
	1b	2b	3b	4b	5b
	1c			4c	5c
					5d

PHSE & C

	PSHEC1 conf & resp	PSHEC2 citizenship	PSHEC3 health	PSHEC4 relationships
	1a	2a	3a	4a
	1b	2b	3b	4b
	1c	2c	3c	4c
	1d	2d	3d	4d
	1e	2e	3e	4e
		2f	3f	
		2g	3g	
		2h		

Art & Design

	A&D1 ideas	A&D2 making	A&D3 evaluating	A&D4 materials	A&D5 breadth
	1a	2a	3a	4a	5a
	1b	2b	3b	4b	5b
		2c		4c	5c
					5d

PE

	PE1 devel skills	PE2 apply skills	PE3 evaluate	PE4 fitness	PE5 breadth
	1a	2a	3a	4a	5a dance
	1b	2b	3b	4b	5b games
		2c	3c		5c gym

Critical skills / Thinking Skills

Critical skills	Thinking Skills
problem solving	observing
decision making	classifying
critical thinking	prediction
creative thinking	making inferences
communication	problem solving
organisation	drawing conclusions
management	
leadership	

Underwater worlds

Underwater world

Previous experience in the Foundation Stage.
Playing with small world and fantasy characters is a favourite for most children, and seems to particularly appeal to boys. in the Early Years Foundation Stage they will probably have:

* used small world figures in water and sand play;
* watched videos and DVDs containing sequences in underwater worlds;
* watched and replayed scenes from superhero movies they have seen on TV or video;
* listened to stories about underwater worlds;
* explored underwater movement and stories in outdoor play, role play and other creative activities.

Pause for thought
In the early stages of working with these materials it is crucial to continue to observe the children. Only by doing this can you set developmentally appropriate challenges and provocations. The ideas listed here are offered as suggestions; the most exciting challenges will arise from children's own interests and motivations, which will only become apparent as you spend time with them, watching and joining them in their play. As you do this, you will be moving between the three interconnecting roles of observer, co-player, extender described below, and will be able to decide what you need to do next to take the learning forward.

The responsive adult (see page 5)

In three interconnecting roles, the responsive adult will be:

* observing
* listening
* interpreting

observer

* **modelling**
* **playing alongside**
* **offering suggestions**
* **responding sensitively**
* **initiating with care!**

co-player

* discussing ideas
* sharing thinking
* modelling new skills
* asking open questions
* being an informed extender
* instigating ideas & thoughts
* supporting children as they make links in learning
* making possibilities evident
* introducing new ideas and resources
* offering challenges and provocations

extender

Offering Challenges and Provocations - some ideas:

In KS1 you could provide small world figures of divers, pirates, mermaids, mermen and other characters such as sea monsters, underwater creatures. Add some plastic bowls and aquariums, aquarium plants and rocks.

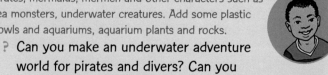

? Can you make an underwater adventure world for pirates and divers? Can you
 - make a story where a pirate ship sinks, the pirates lose their treasure, and it is discovered by divers?
 - photograph your story at various stages to use as a Powerpoint presentation, a photo display or a book?

? Could you make an underwater world for mermaids, mermen and sea monsters. You could make caves with stones and weeds from green or orange plastic carriers cut into leaf shapes. Weight these down by tying the plants to stones. Now make a story about the underwater world.

? Make an information book or poster about underwater worlds. Find some pictures of creatures and habitats by looking on the internet and downloading some photos. Find out about their lives and what they like to eat.

? Set a challenge for your friend. Bury some treasure in an underwater world and let them find the objects. Give them some clues so they know what to look for.

? Google 'Sea-life Adventure' and find out all you can about sharks and tropical fish.

? Find out all you can about the Loch Ness Monster. Now use some Lego to make a monster of your own and make an underwater habitat for it.

? Make a water world for Nemo or The Little Mermaid, or another underwater film.

? Try a superhero underwater scene with Superman, Spiderman or your own favourite superhero.

Ready for more?

- Make some underwater worlds in unusual containers - plastic bottles, bowls, fish tanks or food containers.
- Find out everything you can about Atlantis. Now use plastic construction pieces to make your own version of Atlantis or another underwater city. When you have built your city, find a really big waterproof container and flood your city with water. Take some photos or a video of what you do.
- Write some messages to put in bottles. You could try all sorts and sizes of bottles, just make sure they are plastic, so they float. You could float your bottles in a water tray, an aquarium or down plastic guttering or drainpipes. You could write letters, jokes, questions, challenges, riddles, puzzles or anything else!
- Buy some old crockery from a charity shop. Photograph it, then put it in a strong plastic bag and smash it up. Bury the pieces in an underwater world and see if your friends can use the photos to re-assemble the pieces into the originals.
- Find out about shipwrecks, and make shipwreck scene from recycled materials. Try 'Mary Rose' or 'Titanic' in Google.
- Bury plastic letters, numbers, coins or plastic minibeasts in your underwater world for others to discover.

Materials, equipment suppliers, websites, books and other references

Some ideas for resources and equipment:

Educational suppliers have plenty of small world resources that are ideal for underwater scenes and adventures. Try to collect a range of these that can be offered in small containers or baskets to inspire stories and environments:

- underwater creatures, fish, crabs etc
- small superhero figures, fantasy underwater figures, mermaids and pirates
- underwater monsters and dinosaurs
- models from films such as Finding Nemo or Shark Tale.

There are also lots of free and cheap resources you could collect with the children:

- beads, sequins, jewels and foreign coins
- small boxes and caskets from gifts and other packaging
- buttons, plastic and metal charms, toys from crackers
- small items from aquariums - leaves, plants, buildings
- shells, pebbles and stones, coloured sand and gravel.

Google images: 'underwater', 'sea bed', 'wreck', 'ship in a bottle' which brings up lots of pictures or 'Atlantis' 'mermaid' 'treasure' or 'Loch Ness Monster' will give help with imagined worlds.

Books and Publications:

Summer of the Sea Serpent; (Magic Tree House), Mary Pope Osborne
The Sea Monster; Christopher Wormell; Jonathan Cape
Why Can't I Live Underwater Like the Fish? Sally Hewitt; Belitha Press
A Whale of a Tale; Bonnie Worth; Random House (Cat in the Hat)
Mrs Armitage and the Big Wave; Quentin Blake; Red Fox
Pirates Most Wanted; John Matthews; Atheneum Books
Sinbad the Sailor; Gillian Doherty; Usborne
Master Salt the Sailor; Allan Ahlberg; Puffin Books
Pat the Cat and Sailor Sam; Margaret Wilde; Southwood Books
Sailor Mouse; Peter Curry; Picture Lions
Treasure Island; Robert Louis Stevenson; Audio CD
Pirate Pete; Kim Kennedy; Harry Abrahams

Curriculum coverage grid overleaf

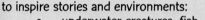

Potential NC KS1 Curriculum Coverage through the provocations suggested for underwater worlds.

Full version of KS1 PoS on pages 69-74
Photocopiable version on page 8

Literacy

	Lit 1 speak	Lit 2 listen	Lit 3 group	Lit 4 drama	Lit 5 word	Lit 6 spell	Lit 7 text1	Lit 8 text2	Lit 9 text3	Lit10 text4	Lit11 sentence	Lit12 presentation
Literacy	1.1	2.1	3.1	4.1	5.1	6.1	7.1	8.1	9.1	10.1	11.1	12.1
	1.2	2.2	3.2	4.2	5.2	6.2	7.2	8.2	9.2	10.2	11.2	12.2

Numeracy

	Num 1 U&A	Num 2 count	Num 3 number	Num 4 calculate	Num 5 shape	Num 6 measure	Num 7 data
Numeracy	1.1	2.1	3.1	4.1	5.1	6.1	7.1
	1.2	2.2	3.2	4.2	5.2	6.2	7.2

Science

	SC1 Enquiry			SC2 Life processes					SC3 Materials		SC4 Phys processes		
	Sc1.1	Sc1.2	Sc1.3	Sc2.1	Sc2.2	Sc2.3	Sc2.4	Sc2.5	Sc3.1	Sc3.2	Sc4.1	Sc4.2	Sc4.3
Science	1.1a	1.2a	1.3a	2.1a	2.2a	2.3a	2.4a	2.5a	3.1a	3.2a	4.1a	4.2a	4.3a
	1.1b	1.2b	1.3b	2.1b	2.2b	2.3b	2.4b	2.5b	3.1b	3.2b	4.1b	4.2b	4.3b
	1.1c	1.2c	1.3c	2.1c	2.2c	2.3c		2.5c	3.1c		4.1c	4.2c	4.3c
	1.1d				2.2d				3.1d				4.3d
					2.2e								
					2.2f								
					2.2g								

ICT

	ICT 1 finding out	ICT 2 ideas	ICT 3 reviewing	ICT 4 breadth
ICT	1.1a	1.2a	2a	3a	4a
	1.1b	1.2b	2b	3b	4b
	1.1c	1.2c	2c	3c	4c
		1.2d			

History

	H1 chronology	H2 events, people	H3 interpret	H4 enquire	H5 org & comm	H6 breadth
History	1a	2a	3a	4a	5a	6a
	1b	2b		4b		6b
						6c
						6d

Geography

	G1.1 & G1.2 enquiry		G2 places	G3 processes	G4 environment	G5 breadth
Geography	1.1a	1.2a	2a	3a	4a	5a
	1.1b	1.2b	2b	3b	4b	5b
	1.1c	1.2c	2c			5c
	1.1d	1.2d	2d			5d
			2e			

D&T

	D&T 1 developing	D&T 2 tool use	D&T 3 evaluating	D&T 4 materials	D&T 5 breadth
D&T	1a	2a	3a	4a	5a
	1b	2b	3b	4b	5b
	1c	2c			5c
	1d	2d			
	1e	2e			

Music

	M1 performing	M2 composing	M3 appraising	M4 listening	M5 breadth
Music	1a	2a	3a	4a	5a
	1b	2b	3b	4b	5b
	1c			4c	5c
					5d

PHSE & C

	PSHEC1 conf & resp	PSHEC2 citizenship	PSHEC3 health	PSHEC4 relationships
PHSE & C	1a	2a	3a	4a
	1b	2b	3b	4b
	1c	2c	3c	4c
	1d	2d	3d	4d
	1e	2e	3e	4e
		2f	3f	
		2g	3g	
		2h		

Art & Design

	A&D1 ideas	A&D2 making	A&D3 evaluating	A&D4 materials	A&D5 breadth
Art & Design	1a	2a	3a	4a	5a
	1b	2b	3b	4b	5b
		2c		4c	5c
					5d

PE

	PE1 devel skills	PE2 apply skills	PE3 evaluate	PE4 fitness	PE5 breadth
PE	1a	2a	3a	4a	5a dance
	1b	2b	3b	4b	5b games
		2c	3c		5c gym

Critical skills	Thinking Skills
problem solving	observing
decision making	classifying
critical thinking	prediction
creative thinking	making inferences
communication	problem solving
organisation	drawing conclusions
management	
leadership	

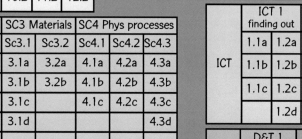

Coloured water

Coloured water

Previous experience in the Foundation Stage.
Changing the colour of water is something that fascinates young children from the earliest age. During the Early Years Foundation Stage they will have explored some of the following:

* free play with coloured and colouring water indoors and outside, with and without tools such as piping, tubes and containers;
* mixing paint;
* adding food colouring to icing, jelly etc;
* changing colours in food, such as making soup, fruit salad, smoothies, juices;
* mixing their own drinks at snack time;
* playing with coloured water and 'tea' in role play;
* experiments with ice, snow, puddle water and other natural materials.

Pause for thought
In the early stages of working with these materials it is crucial to continue to observe the children. Only by doing this can you set developmentally appropriate challenges and provocations. The ideas listed here are offered as suggestions; the most exciting challenges will arise from children's own interests and motivations, which will only become apparent as you spend time with them, watching and joining them in their play. As you do this, you will be moving between the three interconnecting roles of observer, co-player, extender described below, and will be able to decide what you need to do next to take the learning forward.

The responsive adult (see page 5)

In three interconnecting roles, the responsive adult will be:

* observing
* listening
* interpreting

* **modelling**
* **playing alongside**
* **offering suggestions**
* **responding sensitively**
* **initiating with care!**

* discussing ideas
* sharing thinking
* modelling new skills
* asking open questions
* being an informed extender
* instigating ideas & thoughts
* supporting children as they make links in learning
* making possibilities evident
* introducing new ideas and resources
* offering challenges and provocations

Offering Challenges and Provocations - some ideas:

Provide children with all sorts of substances that can colour water - food colouring, paint, fruit and vegetables, tea, coffee, earth, clay etc. Allow plenty of time for free exploration of these substances to see which are most effective. See opposite for some ideas.

? Use the colourings in your classroom to experiment with mixing colours. See how you can make shades of the same colour or new colours. Paint these on paper so you have a record of all the different colours and shades you have made.

? Use some of the colourings you have in your room to make paints. Now make some pictures with the new paints and display them with the colourings you used.

? Use the internet to find out how people made paints, dyes and colourings for fabrics and pictures before they could buy them from shops.

? Use some of this information to make your own dyes and pigments and try them on all sorts of fabrics. Get some old clothes from a charity shop or rummage sale.

? Use the newly dyed fabrics to make decorative hangings or weavings - you could tie them to an old bike wheel, a hoop or some garden netting.

? Find out how to do tie-dye. Now collect the things you need for tie dying some of your own creations. Start with smaller pieces of fabric, then you could decorate your own white teeshirt.

? Batik is another way of decorating fabric. You might have a book in your school that shows you how to do it, or you could put 'batik' into Google and Google Images to find out. Try this method of making patterns on fabric.

? Collect a range of clear plastic containers and fill them with different coloured waters. Put them on a window ledge to make an interesting display.

Ready for more?

- Make a 'giant coloured water' display outside. Use tubes, plastic bottles and containers, and other clear boxes and bowls. Can you make a sculpture with moving water?

- Fill glass bottles with coloured water to make musical bottles. devise a notation system using the colours and compose some bottle music.

- Make some shades of colours using food colouring. Use these shades to paint pictures or patterns.

- Collect some absorbent papers (blotting paper, sugar paper, kitchen roll. Use droppers to make pictures and designs with coloured water.

- Use food colouring on damp paper and watch how the colours behave. can you control the way they do it? Draw some coloured lines on tissues or white kitchen roll with felt pens. Drape the pieces over rulers so the edge JUST touches some water in a bowl. Watch what happens! Dry the paper flat and use it for art work.

- Use food colouring, dyes or paint to colour ice. Freeze the ice in ice cube trays or other containers and then photograph the results. Look carefully at what happens to the colouring when the water freezes.

- get some water-based inks from an art shop and experiment with these. Use them for painting, writing or other marks.

Materials, equipment suppliers, websites, books and other references

Suppliers of equipment and resources:

Batik and tie dye equipment and simple batik techniques available from Fred Aldous www.aldous.co.uk Food dyes (also good for dyeing fabrics and paper) in large quantities, and inks from TTS Group www.tts-group.co.uk

Some fruit and vegetables give cheap dyes - try blackberries (dark blue), onion skins (yellow), beetroot or red plums (dark red). Coffee and tea make easy dyes.

For information on natural dyes try www.thenaturaldyestudio.com or www.pioneerthinking.com/naturaldyes which is a USA site, but has lots of information on what to use and how to prepare the dyes.

Try **Google Images** 'tie dye' 'natural dyes' 'batik' 'natural weaving' 'inks' or 'cave painting' or 'Lascaux' to find out about cave paintings, which were made from mixtures of natural materials or 'Holi' (an Indian festival where everyone gets painted!).

Some Books:

Batik and Tie Dye; Nancy Belfer; Dover Publications
Fabric to Dye for; Susie Stokoe; Southwater
Tie Dye Your Teeshirt; Moira Butterfield; Bloomsbury
Berry Smudges and Leaf Prints; Elaine Senisi; Dutton Books
The Art and Craft of Natural Dyeing; J N Liles; University of Tennessee
A Dyer's Garden; Rita Buchanan; Interweave Press
Wild Colour; Jenny Dean; Mitchell Beazley
Quennu and the Cave Bear; Marie Day; Tandem
Caves of Lascaux; Brad Burnham; Powerkids press
Blackberry Ink (poems); Eve Merriman; William Morrow
Colour (How Artists use...); Paul Flux; Heinemann
Using Colour; Isabelle Thomas; Raintree
Light and Colour; Malcolm Dixon; Evans
Elmer The Elephant; David McKee; Andersen Press

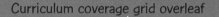

Curriculum coverage grid overleaf

Potential NC KS1 Curriculum Coverage through the provocations suggested for coloured water.

Literacy

	Lit 1 speak	Lit 2 listen	Lit 3 group	Lit 4 drama	Lit 5 word	Lit 6 spell	Lit 7 text1	Lit 8 text2	Lit 9 text3	Lit10 text4	Lit11 sentence	Lit12 presentation
Literacy	1.1	2.1	3.1	4.1	5.1	6.1	7.1	8.1	9.1	10.1	11.1	12.1
	1.2	2.2	3.2	4.2	5.2	6.2	7.2	8.2	9.2	10.2	11.2	12.2

Numeracy

	Num 1 U&A	Num 2 count	Num 3 number	Num 4 calculate	Num 5 shape	Num 6 measure	Num 7 data
Numeracy	1.1	2.1	3.1	4.1	5.1	6.1	7.1
	1.2	2.2	3.2	4.2	5.2	6.2	7.2

Full version of KS1 PoS on pages 69-74
Photocopiable version on page 8

Science

	SC1 Enquiry			SC2 Life processes					SC3 Materials		SC4 Phys processes		
	Sc1.1	Sc1.2	Sc1.3	Sc2.1	Sc2.2	Sc2.3	Sc2.4	Sc2.5	Sc3.1	Sc3.2	Sc4.1	Sc4.2	Sc4.3
Science	1.1a	1.2a	1.3a	2.1a	2.2a	2.3a	2.4a	2.5a	3.1a	3.2a	4.1a	4.2a	4.3a
	1.1b	1.2b	1.3b	2.1b	2.2b	2.3b	2.4b	2.5b	3.1b	3.2b	4.1b	4.2b	4.3b
	1.1c	1.2c	1.3c	2.1c	2.2c	2.3c		2.5c	3.1c		4.1c	4.2c	4.3c
	1.1d				2.2d				3.1d				4.3d
					2.2e								
					2.2f								
					2.2g								

ICT

	ICT 1 finding out		ICT 2 ideas	ICT 3 reviewing	ICT 4 breadth
ICT	1.1a	1.2a	2a	3a	4a
	1.1b	1.2b	2b	3b	4b
	1.1c	1.2c	2c	3c	4c
		1.2d			

History

	H1 chronology	H2 events, people	H3 interpret	H4 enquire	H5 org & comm	H6 breadth
History	1a	2a	3a	4a	5a	6a
	1b	2b		4b		6b
						6c
						6d

Geography

	G1.1 & G1.2 enquiry		G2 places	G3 processes	G4 environment	G5 breadth
Geography	1.1a	1.2a	2a	3a	4a	5a
	1.1b	1.2b	2b	3b	4b	5b
	1.1c	1.2c	2c			5c
	1.1d	1.2d	2d			5d
			2e			

D&T

	D&T 1 developing	D&T 2 tool use	D&T 3 evaluating	D&T 4 materials	D&T 5 breadth
D&T	1a	2a	3a	4a	5a
	1b	2b	3b	4b	5b
	1c	2c			5c
	1d	2d			
	1e	2e			

Music

	M1 performing	M2 composing	M3 appraising	M4 listening	M5 breadth
Music	1a	2a	3a	4a	5a
	1b	2b	3b	4b	5b
	1c			4c	5c
					5d

PHSE & C

	PSHEC1 conf & resp	PSHEC2 citizenship	PSHEC3 health	PSHEC4 relationships
PHSE & C	1a	2a	3a	4a
	1b	2b	3b	4b
	1c	2c	3c	4c
	1d	2d	3d	4d
	1e	2e	3e	4e
		2f	3f	
		2g	3g	
		2h		

Art & Design

	A&D1 ideas	A&D2 making	A&D3 evaluating	A&D4 materials	A&D5 breadth
Art & Design	1a	2a	3a	4a	5a
	1b	2b	3b	4b	5b
		2c		4c	5c
					5d

PE

	PE1 devel skills	PE2 apply skills	PE3 evaluate	PE4 fitness	PE5 breadth
PE	1a	2a	3a	4a	5a dance
	1b	2b	3b	4b	5b games
		2c	3c		5c gym

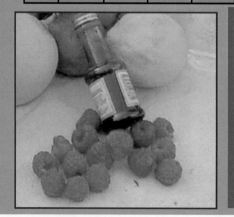

Critical skills	Thinking Skills
problem solving	observing
decision making	classifying
critical thinking	prediction
creative thinking	making inferences
communication	problem solving
organisation	drawing conclusions
management	
leadership	

Adding things

Adding things

Previous experience in the Foundation Stage.
During the early years, children will have experimented widely with adding things to water or water to things. These may have included:
* free play indoors and out of doors;
* making dough;
* cold and hot cooking activities;
* in sand and water play;
* working with clay, dough and other malleable materials;
* making glue and paste;
* mixing paint;
* washing dolls, dolls' clothes, construction toys, vehicles;
* mixing their own drinks.

Pause for thought

In the early stages of working with these materials it is crucial to continue to observe the children. Only by doing this can you set developmentally appropriate challenges and provocations. The ideas listed here are offered as suggestions; the most exciting challenges will arise from children's own interests and motivations, which will only become apparent as you spend time with them, watching and joining them in their play. As you do this, you will be moving between the three interconnecting roles of observer, co-player, extender described below, and will be able to decide what you need to do next to take the learning forward.

The responsive adult (see page 5)

In three interconnecting roles, the responsive adult will be:

* observing
* listening
* interpreting

observer

* **modelling**
* **playing alongside**
* **offering suggestions**
* **responding sensitively**
* **initiating with care!**

co-player

* discussing ideas
* sharing thinking
* modelling new skills
* asking open questions
* being an informed extender
* instigating ideas & thoughts
* supporting children as they make links in learning
* making possibilities evident
* introducing new ideas and resources
* offering challenges and provocations

extender

Offering Challenges and Provocations - some ideas:

NOTE: Encourage children to add objects and substances to water and watch what happens. They may need encouragement from you, and opportunities to select from a wide range of resources to mix and add to plain or coloured water.

? Can you make your own perfume by adding flower petals, herbs, citrus peel etc to water?

? How is bubble bath made? Can you make your own bubble bath from the ingredients in your classroom?

? Make your own sorbets, ice lollies, fruit juices by adding fruit and flavours to water.

? Try mixing cooking oil into water. What happens? Take photos of the different ways you try to make the oil and water mix together.

? Make some fruit drinks with whole fruit, fruit juices and water. Carry out a 'tasting test' and record everyone's favourites. Make a graph of your findings.

? Use flour and water to make your own glue. Experiment with different amounts of flour and water. Test the strength of the glue. What will it sick?

? Make some porridge with different amounts of water to make thin and thick mixtures. Ask your friends to choose if they like thick or thin porridge.

? Collect some different sorts of foods (tea leaves, coffee, salt, sugar, margarine, flour) mix some of each food with water. Which ones dissolve? Think about how you could you get the food out of the water again.

? Mix some icing sugar and water and use this to decorate some biscuits or bought buns.

? Use a runny mixture of icing sugar and water to paint over the surface of some paper. Now use a dropper to drop food colouring on the wet paper. Watch what happens. Take some photos.

Ready for more?

- 🔥 Explore making fizzy water. Use bicarbonate of soda, soluble vitamin tablets or Alka Seltzer tablets. How do they work? Why don't they fizz in the packet?

- 🔥 Find out what happens if you add bicarbonate of soda to water? Make an experiment and take a series of photos of what happens - you may have to do the experiment several times to get the photos! Now make your photos into a worksheet to help other people to do your experiment.

- 🔥 Add straw and mud to water and make your own bricks. What could you use for a mould? Do you want big or small bricks? Leave the bricks to dry and then make a structure or model. Google 'build a mud hut' to find out about Cob houses.

- 🔥 Make bubble mixture with water and washing up liquid. Add a few drops of glycerine to make the bubbles stronger. Now make some of your own bubble blowers from soft wire. Experiment till you find the best one. Take photos of the best and biggest bubbles.

- 🔥 Collect a lot of different recycled materials - plastic, card, paper, fabric. Test these to see which ones dissolve in water and how long it takes. Record your findings.

- 🔥 What happens when vegetables are cooked in boiling water? Look at some raw vegetables and some cooked ones to find out.

Materials, equipment suppliers, websites, books and other references

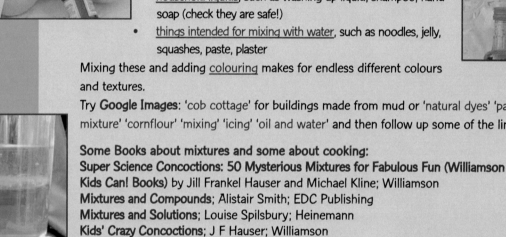

You can add anything to water:
- <u>food substances</u>, such as salt, flour, sugar, icing sugar, cornflour, coffee, tea, vinegar, milk
- <u>natural substances</u>, such as mud, sand, clay, peat, spices, herbs
- <u>natural objects</u>, such as leaves, berries, seeds, petals, stalks, bark, grass
- <u>things that don't mix</u>, such as cooking oils, aromatherapy oils, bath oils
- <u>household liquids</u>, such as washing up liquid, shampoo, hand soap (check they are safe!)
- <u>things intended for mixing with water</u>, such as noodles, jelly, squashes, paste, plaster

Mixing these and adding <u>colouring</u> makes for endless different colours and textures.

Try **Google Images**: 'cob cottage' for buildings made from mud or 'natural dyes' 'paste' 'colour mixture' 'cornflour' 'mixing' 'icing' 'oil and water' and then follow up some of the links.

Some Books about mixtures and some about cooking:
Super Science Concoctions: 50 Mysterious Mixtures for Fabulous Fun (Williamson Kids Can! Books) by Jill Frankel Hauser and Michael Kline; Williamson
Mixtures and Compounds; Alistair Smith; EDC Publishing
Mixtures and Solutions; Louise Spilsbury; Heinemann
Kids' Crazy Concoctions; J F Hauser; Williamson
Snacktivities; MaryAnn Kohl; Roundhouse
Kids Can Cook; Dorothy Bates; Book Publishing Co
No Cook Cookery; Ting Morris; Sea to Sea
Cold Drinks; Ann Redmayne; Evans
Smoothies; Ann Acres Johnson; Klutz
Berry Smudges and Leaf Prints; Ellen Senisi; Dutton
Nature's Playground; Fiona Danks; Chicago Review Press

Curriculum coverage grid overleaf

Potential NC KS1 Curriculum Coverage through the provocations suggested for adding things.

Full version of KS1 PoS on pages 69-74
Photocopiable version on page 8

Literacy

	Lit 1 speak	Lit 2 listen	Lit 3 group	Lit 4 drama	Lit 5 word	Lit 6 spell	Lit 7 text1	Lit 8 text2	Lit 9 text3	Lit10 text4	Lit11 sentence	Lit12 presentation
Literacy	1.1	2.1	3.1	4.1	5.1	6.1	7.1	8.1	9.1	10.1	11.1	12.1
	1.2	2.2	3.2	4.2	5.2	6.2	7.2	8.2	9.2	10.2	11.2	12.2

Numeracy

	Num 1 U&A	Num 2 count	Num 3 number	Num 4 calculate	Num 5 shape	Num 6 measure	Num 7 data
Numeracy	1.1	2.1	3.1	4.1	5.1	6.1	7.1
	1.2	2.2	3.2	4.2	5.2	6.2	7.2

Science

	SC1 Enquiry			SC2 Life processes					SC3 Materials		SC4 Phys processes		
	Sc1.1	Sc1.2	Sc1.3	Sc2.1	Sc2.2	Sc2.3	Sc2.4	Sc2.5	Sc3.1	Sc3.2	Sc4.1	Sc4.2	Sc4.3
Science	1.1a	1.2a	1.3a	2.1a	2.2a	2.3a	2.4a	2.5a	3.1a	3.2a	4.1a	4.2a	4.3a
	1.1b	1.2b	1.3b	2.1b	2.2b	2.3b	2.4b	2.5b	3.1b	3.2b	4.1b	4.2b	4.3b
	1.1c	1.2c	1.3c	2.1c	2.2c	2.3c		2.5c	3.1c		4.1c	4.2c	4.3c
	1.1d				2.2d				3.1d				4.3d
					2.2e								
					2.2f								
					2.2g								

ICT

	ICT 1 finding out		ICT 2 ideas	ICT 3 reviewing	ICT 4 breadth
ICT	1.1a	1.2a	2a	3a	4a
	1.1b	1.2b	2b	3b	4b
	1.1c	1.2c	2c	3c	4c
		1.2d			

D&T

	D&T 1 developing	D&T 2 tool use	D&T 3 evaluating	D&T 4 materials	D&T 5 breadth
D&T	1a	2a	3a	4a	5a
	1b	2b	3b	4b	5b
	1c	2c			5c
	1d	2d			
	1e	2e			

History

	H1 chronology	H2 events, people	H3 interpret	H4 enquire	H5 org & comm	H6 breadth
History	1a	2a	3a	4a	5a	6a
	1b	2b		4b		6b
						6c
						6d

Geography

	G1.1 & G1.2 enquiry		G2 places	G3 processes	G4 environment	G5 breadth
Geography	1.1a	1.2a	2a	3a	4a	5a
	1.1b	1.2b	2b	3b	4b	5b
	1.1c	1.2c	2c			5c
	1.1d	1.2d	2d			5d
			2e			

Music

	M1 performing	M2 composing	M3 appraising	M4 listening	M5 breadth
Music	1a	2a	3a	4a	5a
	1b	2b	3b	4b	5b
	1c			4c	5c
					5d

PSHE & C

	PSHEC1 conf & resp	PSHEC2 citizenship	PSHEC3 health	PSHEC4 relationships
PHSE & C	1a	2a	3a	4a
	1b	2b	3b	4b
	1c	2c	3c	4c
	1d	2d	3d	4d
	1e	2e	3e	4e
		2f	3f	
		2g	3g	
		2h		

Art & Design

	A&D1 ideas	A&D2 making	A&D3 evaluating	A&D4 materials	A&D5 breadth
Art & Design	1a	2a	3a	4a	5a
	1b	2b	3b	4b	5b
		2c		4c	5c
					5d

PE

	PE1 devel skills	PE2 apply skills	PE3 evaluate	PE4 fitness	PE5 breadth
PE	1a	2a	3a	4a	5a dance
	1b	2b	3b	4b	5b games
		2c	3c		5c gym

Critical skills	Thinking Skills
problem solving	observing
decision making	classifying
critical thinking	prediction
creative thinking	making inferences
communication	problem solving
organisation	drawing conclusions
management	
leadership	

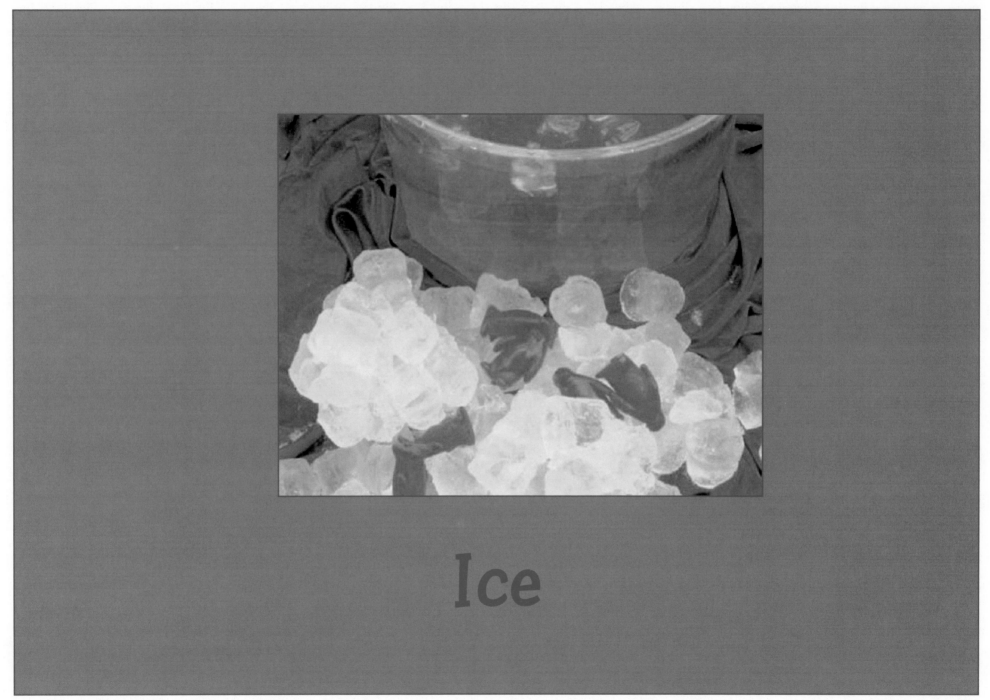

Ice

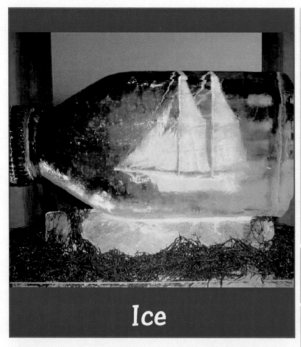

Ice

Previous experience in the Foundation Stage.

Most children will have had experience of naturally occurring ice, but even this is a less frequent event with climate change and safety concerns. Some children will have:

* played with ice at home;
* experienced watching ice in drinks;
* made ice lollies;
* played with ice shapes and cubes in water trays;
* explored ice in puddles, ditches and ponds.

Pause for thought

In the early stages of working with these materials it is crucial to continue to observe the children. Only by doing this can you set developmentally appropriate challenges and provocations. The ideas listed here are offered as suggestions; the most exciting challenges will arise from children's own interests and motivations, which will only become apparent as you spend time with them, watching and joining them in their play. As you do this, you will be moving between the three interconnecting roles of observer, co-player, extender described below, and will be able to decide what you need to do next to take the learning forward.

The responsive adult (see page 5)

In three interconnecting roles, the responsive adult will be:

* observing
* listening
* interpreting

observer

* **modelling**
* **playing alongside**
* **offering suggestions**
* **responding sensitively**
* **initiating with care!**

co-player

* discussing ideas
* sharing thinking
* modelling new skills
* asking open questions
* being an informed extender
* instigating ideas & thoughts
* supporting children as they make links in learning
* making possibilities evident
* introducing new ideas and resources
* offering challenges and provocations

extender

Offering Challenges and Provocations - some ideas:

NOTE: Children will need to explore ice in free play before using it in experiments or adult directed activities. Try just offering a bag of ice cubes (either bought from a supermarket or made yourself). Tip it into a bowl or onto a builder's tray for free play. Offer gloves if children need them - most won't want them! - and warn them not to eat the cubes.

? How high can you build with the ice cubes? Are they easy to build with?

? Can you build an igloo with the ice cubes?

? Find some small world figures (polar bears, penguins, eskimos etc) and make an environment for them with the ice cubes.

? Put one ice cube on a table, one outside the door and one in your hand. Which one melts first? Do you know why this happens? Try the same experiment with a few friends - each holding a cube in their hand.

NOTE: These challenges need access to a freezer or ice making compartment of a fridge.

? Fill some plastic containers, cups, yoghurt pots, margarine tubs with water. Use a dropper to add a few drops of food colouring to each container. Put the containers in the freezer overnight. Tip the ice out and see what has happened. Take some photos.

? Try making ice shapes in unusual containers - a rubber glove, a wellington boot, a beach bucket shaped like a castle, a plastic bag tied at the top. Use coloured water if you like.

? Fill a bowl with cold water and tip some ice cubes or ice shapes in the water. What happens to the ice cubes? Take just six photos to show what happens over time. You will need to think about when you take them! Make a display of your findings.

? Make some ice lollies with fruit juice and water.

Ready for more?

- Find an ice cube tray. Put small things in each of the sections - beads, sequins, little pictures, buttons, coins. Fill the tray with water or coloured water and freeze it. Tip the cubes out when they have frozen. Now look up 'ice cube scramble' in Google Images and click through to information about an Ice Cube Scramble in America where children scramble for ice cubes with toys and tokens inside.
- Go outside and collect some leaves, twigs, petals, small flowers, seeds. Now find some shallow containers - lids, plastic trays, polystyrene trays. Make patterns with your natural objects and very gently fill the container with water. Add a piece of string or ribbon to the edge (so you can hang it up) and freeze your pattern. When it is frozen, take it out of the container and hang it up out of doors.
- Try the same method with bird food and other seeds and hang it up in winter for the birds to peck at.
- Look up 'ice sculpture' in Google Images and see what you can find. Some of the images on this page come from www.icechef.com - see what else he has made. The goldfish are real and they are swimming in real water!
- Try making a frozen fish tank with some plastic fish and weeds made from green plastic strips in green water, then freeze it.

Materials, equipment suppliers, websites, books and other references

www.icechef.com

Access to a freezer or fridge is fairly essential, but you could make ice shapes at home, or encourage the children to do so. If you need to transport them, use a freezer bag, or ice packs, or just wrap the ice in a thick layer of newspaper or a blanket and put it in a plastic bag. It should stay frozen for at least an hour. If the children experiment with unusual ice moulds at home, they could leave the ice in these and bring it to school before they tip it out.

Most supermarkets sell ice cubes in bags. They cost under a pound for a big bag, and they are suitable for all sorts of experiments.

Get ice packs from www.lakeland.co.uk or your local supermarket, and try Pound Shops for unusual ice cube trays and drink coolers (shapes to freeze to drop in drinks, like the penguins below).

Look at www.icechef.com for some wonderful examples of ice carving and photos of the ice chef at work, or Google Ice Festivals for some great pictures from the BBC of the Japanese Ice Festival. www.blackjackbuffers.com has photos of Russian ice sculptures and www.thisisthelife.com has ice sculptures in Alaska.

www.icechef.com

Google Images responds well to 'icicle' 'icicle lights' 'ice cube moulds' and some inspiration may come by trying 'ice sculpture' 'igloo' 'ice cave' 'glacier' and 'iceberg'. Also try www.iceicleinn.com where there is an ice cube scramble for kids that might be worth replicating in school!

Andy Goldsworthy, the sculptor has had some fun with big snowballs - try Andy Goldsworthy snowballs in Google

Books and Stories:
Matsumara's Ice Sculpture: Prokos; Longman
 Ice and Snow Drawings; Andy Goldsworthy; Fruitmarket Gallery
 Winter Nature Activities for Children; Dagmar Israel; Floris Books
 Nature's Playground; Fiona Danks; Frances Lincoln
 Building and Igloo; Ulli Steltzer; Henry Holt

Curriculum coverage grid overleaf

www.icechef.com

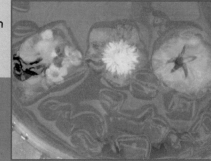

Literacy

	Lit 1 speak	Lit 2 listen	Lit 3 group	Lit 4 drama	Lit 5 word	Lit 6 spell	Lit 7 text1	Lit 8 text2	Lit 9 text3	Lit10 text4	Lit11 sentence	Lit12 presentation
Literacy	1.1	2.1	3.1	4.1	5.1	6.1	7.1	8.1	9.1	10.1	11.1	12.1
	1.2	2.2	3.2	4.2	5.2	6.2	7.2	8.2	9.2	10.2	11.2	12.2

Numeracy

	Num 1 U&A	Num 2 count	Num 3 number	Num 4 calculate	Num 5 shape	Num 6 measure	Num 7 data
Numeracy	1.1	2.1	3.1	4.1	5.1	6.1	7.1
	1.2	2.2	3.2	4.2	5.2	6.2	7.2

Science

	SC1 Enquiry			SC2 Life processes					SC3 Materials		SC4 Phys processes		
	Sc1.1	Sc1.2	Sc1.3	Sc2.1	Sc2.2	Sc2.3	Sc2.4	Sc2.5	Sc3.1	Sc3.2	Sc4.1	Sc4.2	Sc4.3
Science	1.1a	1.2a	1.3a	2.1a	2.2a	2.3a	2.4a	2.5a	3.1a	3.2a	4.1a	4.2a	4.3a
	1.1b	1.2b	1.3b	2.1b	2.2b	2.3b	2.4b	2.5b	3.1b	3.2b	4.1b	4.2b	4.3b
	1.1c	1.2c	1.3c	2.1c	2.2c	2.3c		2.5c	3.1c		4.1c	4.2c	4.3c
	1.1d				2.2d				3.1d				4.3d
					2.2e								
					2.2f								
					2.2g								

ICT

	ICT 1 finding out		ICT 2 ideas	ICT 3 reviewing	ICT 4 breadth
ICT	1.1a	1.2a	2a	3a	4a
	1.1b	1.2b	2b	3b	4b
	1.1c	1.2c	2c	3c	4c
		1.2d			

D&T

	D&T 1 developing	D&T 2 tool use	D&T 3 evaluating	D&T 4 materials	D&T 5 breadth
D&T	1a	2a	3a	4a	5a
	1b	2b	3b	4b	5b
	1c	2c			5c
	1d	2d			
	1e	2e			

History

	H1 chronology	H2 events, people	H3 interpret	H4 enquire	H5 org & comm	H6 breadth
History	1a	2a	3a	4a	5a	6a
	1b	2b		4b		6b
						6c
						6d

Geography

	G1.1 & G1.2 enquiry		G2 places	G3 processes	G4 environment	G5 breadth
Geography	1.1a	1.2a	2a	3a	4a	5a
	1.1b	1.2b	2b	3b	4b	5b
	1.1c	1.2c	2c			5c
	1.1d	1.2d	2d			5d
			2e			

Music

	M1 performing	M2 composing	M3 appraising	M4 listening	M5 breadth
Music	1a	2a	3a	4a	5a
	1b	2b	3b	4b	5b
	1c			4c	5c
					5d

PHSE & C

	PSHEC1 conf & resp	PSHEC2 citizenship	PSHEC3 health	PSHEC4 relationships
PHSE & C	1a	2a	3a	4a
	1b	2b	3b	4b
	1c	2c	3c	4c
	1d	2d	3d	4d
	1e	2e	3e	4e
		2f	3f	
		2g	3g	
		2h		

Art & Design

	A&D1 ideas	A&D2 making	A&D3 evaluating	A&D4 materials	A&D5 breadth
Art & Design	1a	2a	3a	4a	5a
	1b	2b	3b	4b	5b
		2c		4c	5c
					5d

PE

	PE1 devel skills	PE2 apply skills	PE3 evaluate	PE4 fitness	PE5 breadth
PE	1a	2a	3a	4a	5a dance
	1b	2b	3b	4b	5b games
		2c	3c		5c gym

Critical skills	Thinking Skills
problem solving	observing
decision making	classifying
critical thinking	prediction
creative thinking	making inferences
communication	problem solving
organisation	drawing conclusions
management	
leadership	

Full version of KS1 PoS on pages 69-74
Photocopiable version on page 8

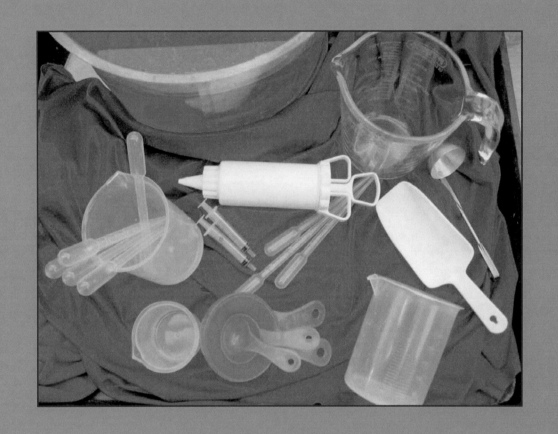

Measuring water

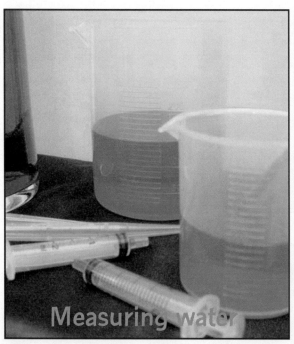

Measuring water

Previous experience in the Foundation Stage.

Jugs, measuring beakers and cups are familiar equipment in the Foundation Stage, and most children will have done some experimenting:

* in free play indoors and outside;
* with filling and emptying;
* in stacking and nesting different sizes of containers;
* in scooping, pouring, ladling and tipping liquids and solids such as sand.

Pause for thought
In the early stages of working with these materials it is crucial to continue to observe the children. Only by doing this can you set developmentally appropriate challenges and provocations. The ideas listed here are offered as suggestions; the most exciting challenges will arise from children's own interests and motivations, which will only become apparent as you spend time with them, watching and joining them in their play. As you do this, you will be moving between the three interconnecting roles of observer, co-player, extender described below, and will be able to decide what you need to do next to take the learning forward.

The responsive adult (see page 5)

In three interconnecting roles, the responsive adult will be:

* observing
* listening
* interpreting

observer

* **modelling**
* **playing alongside**
* **offering suggestions**
* **responding sensitively**
* **initiating with care!**

co-player

* discussing ideas
* sharing thinking
* modelling new skills
* asking open questions
* being an informed extender
* instigating ideas & thoughts
* supporting children as they make links in learning
* making possibilities evident
* introducing new ideas and resources
* offering challenges and provocations

extender

Offering Challenges and Provocations - some ideas:

? Find some recycled containers of different sizes (yoghurt pots, milk, water or juice bottles etc). Now estimate which one holds most, which holds least. Put them in the order you think, and take a photo. Now use water find out the capacity of each container. After your experiment, put the containers in the order of their capacity and take another photo. Were you right?

? Get some spoons of different sizes and three containers of different sizes. Can you use these to find out how many spoonfuls each container holds? Use your brain and plan well. You may find a clever way to do it!

? Get an egg cup, a plastic cup and a bucket. Use these to find out how many egg cups of water fill the bucket. Work with a friend to think and plan before you start.

? Find some recycled containers with printing on them. Look for the place where the amount of the contents is written. It will say something like 4fl oz (120ml). Put the containers in order of their capacity. Is this the same as the order of their size?

? Now use these containers to check for accuracy. For this investigation you need some plastic beakers with measurements marked on them. Use these to check the capacity of the containers you found, to see if the labelling is accurate. What do you find? Why could this be?

? Find a plastic water bottle. Can you make your own measuring beaker from this, using a permanent marker? take some photos of all the different stages of making your measuring beaker.

- Use the internet or a book to find out about litres (l), centilitres (cl) and millilitres (ml). Now use the methods you found for making beakers from recycled materials to make measuring beakers of different sizes. Try to find different sized containers for the different capacities, and mark them with a permanent marker.

- Fill some plastic beakers with water to the top measurement level. Now try dropping objects gently into the beakers. What happens to the water level? Why might this be? Does the same thing happen with every object you put in? Try using pebbles, Lego bricks, conkers, coins. What happens if you use ice cubes?

- Now use what you found out to calculate how much space the following things take in water:

    6 Lego bricks
    14 pebbles
    an empty water bottle
    a full water bottle
    4 Play people

    record what you find out.

- Do the same investigation with a house brick. Put water in a bowl and measure the surface level. Put the brick in carefully and measure the level again. Wait ten minutes and measure again. What has happened? Why do you think that is?

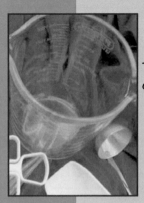

TIP:
A litre of water
weighs exactly one
kilogram

Materials, equipment, suppliers, websites, books and other references

Try to collect as many different sorts of containers and measuring vessels as you can. They could be:

Recycled containers such as yoghurt pots, plastic spoons, water bottles, juice bottles, plastic containers from milk, washing up liquid, detergents

Kitchen equipment (try bargain shops, charity shops and markets) such as plastic jugs, measuring spoons, scoops

Science equipment such as measuring beakers, measuring spoons, pipettes, plastic test tubes and funnels

Don't forget to add some very small containers, such as those from perfumes, aromatherapy oils and spices.

If you can afford to buy something from an educational supplier, try www.new.craftpacks.co.uk for measuring beakers, or ask your science co-ordinator for the address of their suppliers. Many educational suppliers' catalogues have water measuring equipment, sometimes the Early Years section is best for finding equipment for KS1 children to use independently. Add some tubing and funnels, and get some very small funnels from aromatherapy oil suppliers. www.metric.org.uk/whatis/definitions has useful conversion charts for liquids and solids, such as - 1 litre = 10 décilitres = 100 centilitres = 1000 millilitres,

Try **Google Images** 'measuring containers' or 'measuring jugs' 'funnel' 'measuring spoons'.

Some books:

Capacity; Henry Pluckrose; Franklin Watts

Measuring; Ruth Merttens; Scholastic

Measuring: Key Stage 1; Barbara Raper; Scholastic

Rain and Snow, measuring the weather; Heinemann

Starting Off with Measuring; Peter Patilla; OUP

Measuring (Start Maths); Ann Montague-Smith; QED

Curriculum coverage grid overleaf

Potential NC KS1 Curriculum Coverage through the provocations suggested for measuring water.

Literacy

	Lit 1 speak	Lit 2 listen	Lit 3 group	Lit 4 drama	Lit 5 word	Lit 6 spell	Lit 7 text1	Lit 8 text2	Lit 9 text3	Lit10 text4	Lit11 sentence	Lit12 presentation
Literacy	1.1	2.1	3.1	4.1	5.1	6.1	7.1	8.1	9.1	10.1	11.1	12.1
	1.2	2.2	3.2	4.2	5.2	6.2	7.2	8.2	9.2	10.2	11.2	12.2

Numeracy

	Num 1 U&A	Num 2 count	Num 3 number	Num 4 calculate	Num 5 shape	Num 6 measure	Num 7 data
Numeracy	1.1	2.1	3.1	4.1	5.1	6.1	7.1
	1.2	2.2	3.2	4.2	5.2	6.2	7.2

Full version of KS1 PoS on pages 69-74
Photocopiable version on page 8

Science

	SC1 Enquiry			SC2 Life processes					SC3 Materials		SC4 Phys processes		
	Sc1.1	Sc1.2	Sc1.3	Sc2.1	Sc2.2	Sc2.3	Sc2.4	Sc2.5	Sc3.1	Sc3.2	Sc4.1	Sc4.2	Sc4.3
Science	1.1a	1.2a	1.3a	2.1a	2.2a	2.3a	2.4a	2.5a	3.1a	3.2a	4.1a	4.2a	4.3a
	1.1b	1.2b	1.3b	2.1b	2.2b	2.3b	2.4b	2.5b	3.1b	3.2b	4.1b	4.2b	4.3b
	1.1c	1.2c	1.3c	2.1c	2.2c	2.3c		2.5c	3.1c		4.1c	4.2c	4.3c
	1.1d				2.2d				3.1d				4.3d
					2.2e								
					2.2f								
					2.2g								

ICT

	ICT 1 finding out	ICT 2 ideas	ICT 3 reviewing	ICT 4 breadth
ICT	1.1a / 1.2a	2a	3a	4a
	1.1b / 1.2b	2b	3b	4b
	1.1c / 1.2c	2c	3c	4c
	1.2d			

History

	H1 chronology	H2 events, people	H3 interpret	H4 enquire	H5 org & comm	H6 breadth
History	1a	2a	3a	4a	5a	6a
	1b	2b		4b		6b
						6c
						6d

Geography

	G1.1 & G1.2 enquiry		G2 places	G3 processes	G4 environment	G5 breadth
Geography	1.1a	1.2a	2a	3a	4a	5a
	1.1b	1.2b	2b	3b	4b	5b
	1.1c	1.2c	2c			5c
	1.1d	1.2d	2d			5d
			2e			

D&T

	D&T 1 developing	D&T 2 tool use	D&T 3 evaluating	D&T 4 materials	D&T 5 breadth
D&T	1a	2a	3a	4a	5a
	1b	2b	3b	4b	5b
	1c	2c			5c
	1d	2d			
	1e	2e			

Music

	M1 performing	M2 composing	M3 appraising	M4 listening	M5 breadth
Music	1a	2a	3a	4a	5a
	1b	2b	3b	4b	5b
	1c			4c	5c
					5d

PHSE & C

	PSHEC1 conf & resp	PSHEC2 citizenship	PSHEC3 health	PSHEC4 relationships
PHSE & C	1a	2a	3a	4a
	1b	2b	3b	4b
	1c	2c	3c	4c
	1d	2d	3d	4d
	1e	2e	3e	4e
		2f	3f	
		2g	3g	
		2h		

Art & Design

	A&D1 ideas	A&D2 making	A&D3 evaluating	A&D4 materials	A&D5 breadth
Art & Design	1a	2a	3a	4a	5a
	1b	2b	3b	4b	5b
		2c		4c	5c
					5d

PE

	PE1 devel skills	PE2 apply skills	PE3 evaluate	PE4 fitness	PE5 breadth
PE	1a	2a	3a	4a	5a dance
	1b	2b	3b	4b	5b games
		2c	3c		5c gym

Critical skills	Thinking Skills
problem solving	observing
decision making	classifying
critical thinking	prediction
creative thinking	making inferences
communication	problem solving
organisation	drawing conclusions
management	
leadership	

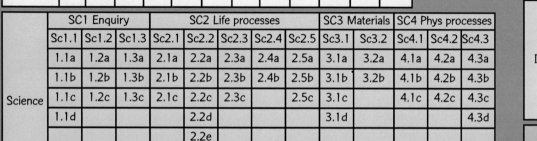

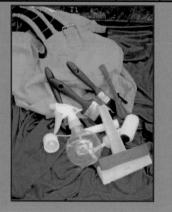

Divers and diving

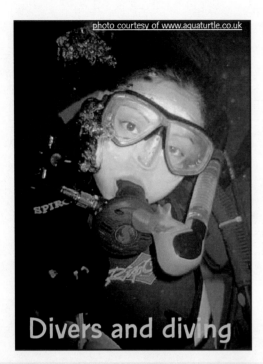

photo courtesy of www.aquaturtle.co.uk

Divers and diving

Previous experience in the Foundation Stage.
In the Foundation Stage, children may have had experience of using toy divers in water play, in role play, or they may have experimented with underwater swimming. These experiences might have been:

* in small world play;
* in experiments and observations;
* in full role play with flippers and goggles;
* while on holiday in swimming pools and the sea;
* watching underwater films on DVD or film;
* experimenting with submerging things such as water bottles in water play.

Pause for thought

In the early stages of working with these materials it is crucial to continue to observe the children. Only by doing this can you set developmentally appropriate challenges and provocations. The ideas listed here are offered as suggestions; the most exciting challenges will arise from children's own interests and motivations, which will only become apparent as you spend time with them, watching and joining them in their play. As you do this, you will be moving between the three interconnecting roles of observer, co-player, extender described below, and will be able to decide what you need to do next to take the learning forward.

The responsive adult (see page 5)

In three interconnecting roles, the responsive adult will be:

* observing
* listening
* interpreting

observer

* **modelling**
* **playing alongside**
* **offering suggestions**
* **responding sensitively**
* **initiating with care!**

co-player

* discussing ideas
* sharing thinking
* modelling new skills
* asking open questions
* being an informed extender
* instigating ideas & thoughts
* supporting children as they make links in learning
* making possibilities evident
* introducing new ideas and resources
* offering challenges and provocations

extender

Offering Challenges and Provocations - some ideas:

? Use water bottles to experiment with making submarines. How can you make them sink? Can you make them come up again?

? Why do humans need face masks and snorkels? Find out from the internet or books.

? Can you make a mask and snorkel from recycled materials? Why won't this work in a real swimming pool?

? Find some plastic tubing and experiment with blowing bubbles like a diver. What happens if you suck? Why does the end of a diver's snorkel stick up out of the water?

? Find out how long you can hold your breath for. Sit or lie down while you do this test, because it may make you feel dizzy! Who can hold their breath for the longest? Use a stopwatch to find out.

? Find some small world people or superheroes. Can you make a diving bell or submarine for them to travel in?

? Make a marine habitat for your submarine in an aquarium or water tray, using rocks, shells, plastic aquarium plants and other objects.

? Float a sponge on the surface of some water. Can you make the sponge sink? How did you do it?

? Tie a small world person or a superhero figure on a piece of string. Now dip it in a bowl or bucket of water. What happens? How can you make the figure sink to the bottom of the water? and how can you make it come up again? Think carefully about what you can use to weight the figure. Try several different ways. Which works best?

? Find out about the Great Diving Beetle www.arkive.org. How does this beetle breathe underwater? Look up water diving beetles on the internet. Make a fact sheet of the things you find out. Get someone to help you to download some photos or drawings.

Ready for more?

- Some insects and animals can hold their breath for a long time - look in books and on the internet to find out about beavers, otters, whales, turtles, hippos and others. How many different animals can you find that usually live on land, but can swim underwater?

- Can you find out how a real submarine works? Do a labelled drawing of this so you can explain it to someone else.

- How do divers' flippers work? Look at some pictures of divers and of big fish. Can you see how the flippers work to make the diver swim faster?

- Look on the internet at: www.kids-science-experiments.com Find the floating and sinking experiments and find out how to make a toy diver from a pen top and some Plasticine. Make several of these divers with your friends and see which one is best.

- Try some more experiments from this site and from other sites you find when you Google 'science experiments kids'.

- See if you can find a cheap diving toy in a toy shop. Does it work in the same way as the diver you made?

- Go to www.psbkids.org and find the experiment called Dancing Raisins. Collect the things you need (from home or school) and try this experiment with a friend. What makes the raisins dance?

Materials, equipment suppliers, websites, books and other references

Suppliers: www.amazon.co.uk supply all the toy submarines shown on these pages. You can also get divers from toy catalogues and hundreds of websites selling toys.

Try www.kids-science-experiments.com for experiments in floating and sinking, or Google simple science experiments diver for kids experiments and how to make divers from simple objects.

Collect bottles and small plastic containers for experiments, and offer plastic fish tanks or washing up bowls for trials.

The diving photos on these pages can be found on www.aquaturtle.co.uk a diving school for kids.

Try **Google Images:** 'diver' 'submarine' 'underwater' 'scuba diving' 'tropical fish' 'sub-aqua' 'Jacques Cousteau'.

Some **books:**
What's under the Sea?; Sophie Tahta; Usborne
Snail and the Whale; Julia Donaldson; Macmillan
Dougal's Deep-sea Diary (Paperback); by Simon Bartram; Templar
Lemmy Was a Diver; Colin McNaughton; Andersen
The Pearl Diver; Julia Johnson; Stacey International
Why Can't I Live Underwater with the Fish; sally Hewitt; Belitha Press
Four Corners, Underwater Treasures; Maureen Haselhurst; Longman
Underwater World; Angela Wilkes; Two-Can
One Night in the Coral Sea; B Sneer; Charlesbridge Publishing
Inside a Coral Reef; Carole Telford; Heinemann
Coral Reef; Caroline Bingham; DK
This is the Reef; Miriam Moss; Frances Lincoln
Over in the Ocean; In a Coral Reef; Marianne Berks; Dawn Publications
Submarine; Neil Mallard; DK
Commotion in the Ocean; Giles Andreae; Orchard Books

photo courtesy of www.aquaturtle.co.uk

photo courtesy of www.aquaturtle.co.uk

Potential NC KS1 Curriculum Coverage through the provocations suggested for divers and diving.

Literacy

	Lit 1 speak	Lit 2 listen	Lit 3 group	Lit 4 drama	Lit 5 word	Lit 6 spell	Lit 7 text1	Lit 8 text2	Lit 9 text3	Lit10 text4	Lit11 sentence	Lit12 presentation
	1.1	2.1	3.1	4.1	5.1	6.1	7.1	8.1	9.1	10.1	11.1	12.1
	1.2	2.2	3.2	4.2	5.2	6.2	7.2	8.2	9.2	10.2	11.2	12.2

Numeracy

	Num 1 U&A	Num 2 count	Num 3 number	Num 4 calculate	Num 5 shape	Num 6 measure	Num 7 data
	1.1	2.1	3.1	4.1	5.1	6.1	7.1
	1.2	2.2	3.2	4.2	5.2	6.2	7.2

Full version of KS1 PoS on pages 69-74
Photocopiable version on page 8

Science

	SC1 Enquiry			SC2 Life processes					SC3 Materials		SC4 Phys processes		
	Sc1.1	Sc1.2	Sc1.3	Sc2.1	Sc2.2	Sc2.3	Sc2.4	Sc2.5	Sc3.1	Sc3.2	Sc4.1	Sc4.2	Sc4.3
	1.1a	1.2a	1.3a	2.1a	2.2a	2.3a	2.4a	2.5a	3.1a	3.2a	4.1a	4.2a	4.3a
	1.1b	1.2b	1.3b	2.1b	2.2b	2.3b	2.4b	2.5b	3.1b	3.2b	4.1b	4.2b	4.3b
	1.1c	1.2c	1.3c	2.1c	2.2c	2.3c		2.5c	3.1c		4.1c	4.2c	4.3c
	1.1d				2.2d				3.1d				4.3d
					2.2e								
					2.2f								
					2.2g								

ICT

	ICT 1 finding out		ICT 2 ideas	ICT 3 reviewing	ICT 4 breadth
	1.1a	1.2a	2a	3a	4a
	1.1b	1.2b	2b	3b	4b
	1.1c	1.2c	2c	3c	4c
		1.2d			

D&T

	D&T 1 developing	D&T 2 tool use	D&T 3 evaluating	D&T 4 materials	D&T 5 breadth
	1a	2a	3a	4a	5a
	1b	2b	3b	4b	5b
	1c	2c			5c
	1d	2d			
	1e	2e			

History

	H1 chronology	H2 events, people	H3 interpret	H4 enquire	H5 org & comm	H6 breadth
	1a	2a	3a	4a	5a	6a
	1b	2b		4b		6b
						6c
						6d

Geography

	G1.1 & G1.2 enquiry		G2 places	G3 processes	G4 environment	G5 breadth
	1.1a	1.2a	2a	3a	4a	5a
	1.1b	1.2b	2b	3b	4b	5b
	1.1c	1.2c	2c			5c
	1.1d	1.2d	2d			5d
			2e			

Music

	M1 performing	M2 composing	M3 appraising	M4 listening	M5 breadth
	1a	2a	3a	4a	5a
	1b	2b	3b	4b	5b
	1c			4c	5c
					5d

PHSE & C

	PSHEC1 conf & resp	PSHEC2 citizenship	PSHEC3 health	PSHEC4 relationships
	1a	2a	3a	4a
	1b	2b	3b	4b
	1c	2c	3c	4c
	1d	2d	3d	4d
	1e	2e	3e	4e
		2f	3f	
		2g	3g	
		2h		

Art & Design

	A&D1 ideas	A&D2 making	A&D3 evaluating	A&D4 materials	A&D5 breadth
	1a	2a	3a	4a	5a
	1b	2b	3b	4b	5b
		2c		4c	5c
					5d

PE

	PE1 devel skills	PE2 apply skills	PE3 evaluate	PE4 fitness	PE5 breadth
	1a	2a	3a	4a	5a dance
	1b	2b	3b	4b	5b games
		2c	3c		5c gym

Critical skills	Thinking Skills
problem solving	observing
decision making	classifying
critical thinking	prediction
creative thinking	making inferences
communication	problem solving
organisation	drawing conclusions
management	
leadership	

photo courtesy of www.aquaturtle.co.uk

Jelly and other additions

Jelly and additions

Previous experience in the Foundation Stage.
Throughout their time in the Early Years Foundation Stage, children will have been involved in jelly making. They may have:

* helped to make jelly for parties or to eat at snack time;
* played with jelly in the sand and water trays;
* explored the properties of jelly in early science and language activities;
* explored the language and vocabulary of describing jelly and how it looks, behaves and feels;
* used jelly to make landscapes and environments for small world play;
* mixed objects and small toys with jelly and watched them set;
* used moulds to make jelly shapes.

Pause for thought

In the early stages of working with these materials it is crucial to continue to observe the children. Only by doing this can you set developmentally appropriate challenges and provocations. The ideas listed here are offered as suggestions; the most exciting challenges will arise from children's own interests and motivations, which will only become apparent as you spend time with them, watching and joining them in their play. As you do this, you will be moving between the three interconnecting roles of observer, co-player, extender described below, and will be able to decide what you need to do next to take the learning forward.

The responsive adult (see page 5)

In three interconnecting roles, the responsive adult will be:

* observing
* listening
* interpreting

observer

* **modelling**
* **playing alongside**
* **offering suggestions**
* **responding sensitively**
* **initiating with care!**

co-player

* discussing ideas
* sharing thinking
* modelling new skills
* asking open questions
* being an informed extender
* instigating ideas & thoughts
* supporting children as they make links in learning
* making possibilities evident
* introducing new ideas and resources
* offering challenges and provocations

extender

Offering Challenges and Provocations - some ideas:

NOTE: Some of these provocations will need preparation, but once children get used to the properties of jelly, they can do the preparation as part of the activity, or prepare things for others.

? Make a jelly with small fruit or objects in it. Now get your friends to guess and write down how many raspberries, blueberries, fish, marbles are set in your jelly. Now find out and count them to check (you will have to take them out of the jelly!). Who was right? Who was nearest? Set up a new challenge with some more jelly and objects. Make sure you can see the objects by using transparent containers.

? Use jelly to create:
   - a lunar landscape
   - a swamp
   - a dinosaur world
   - a fairy forest

Add small world figures, leaves and twigs, stones and pebbles to your world. Now make up a story and take photos of each scene. Make a book or a Powerpoint presentation for your friends to look at.

? Make some different shaped small jellies in pots or moulds. Use these to make a sculpture. Make sure you take some photos to preserve your work of art!

? Can you make a striped jelly with more than one colour! How can you do this?

? When you know how to make a striped jelly, make one where the stripes are:
   - uneven widths or
   - sloping or
   - vertical.

Record how you did it, so your friends can do it too. Make a display or book of your instructions and photos with your jellies.

Ready for more?

- Bury items in chopped up jelly and set up a treasure hunt for your friends. Make a chart showing all the objects and see how long it takes to find them all. Have some VERY tiny objects to make the challenge even more difficult, but make sure they aren't things that dissolve!

- Make lots of small jellies in yogurt pots or the supermarket plastic trays that yoghurts come in. Now see if you can make towers with the set jellies. How high can you build?

- Make a 'designer' jelly. Add fruit and berries, 'hundreds and thousands' and other edible cake decorations. Eat your jelly at snack time.

- Can you make a savoury jelly? You need some gelatin and small pieces of vegetable - cucumber, cherry tomatoes, celery, peas etc. You can even add cooked pasta shapes.

- Make some jellies and when they are set, guess which is heaviest by holding them in your hand. Put them in order from heaviest to lightest. Now weigh them to check your estimates and predictions.

- Try making your own jellies from plain gelatin and fruit juices. Add some pieces of fruit to make them taste even better.

- Use food colouring to make unusual colour of jelly - black, brown or purple.

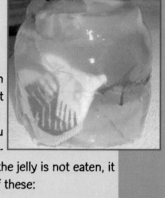

Materials, equipment suppliers, websites, books and other references

Suppliers and sources:

Jelly is a really cheap substance to experiment with. Buy bargain versions as long as you don't want the children to eat it, but check for additives and colourings if you do!

There are hundreds of different containers and jelly moulds you can use to set the jellies in. Transparent containers make it easier to see what is going on, and for some experiments where the jelly is not eaten, it doesn't matter if you can't get the jelly out again. Try some of these:

- plastic cups, mugs and bowls
- water bottles with the tops cut off
- yoghurt pots and margarine tubs
- vases and pots for flowers and plants
- liners from jam tarts, chocolates, jelly sweet boxes, food trays
- sand and clay moulds
- biscuit and cake moulds
- commercial jelly moulds

Use Google Images for pictures - some suggestions for words to search: 'jelly' 'jelly moulds' 'jelly babies' 'jelly sculpture' 'rowntrees jelly'.

www.aquarterof.co.uk is a site about sweets where you can look for details of all sorts of sweets, including jelly babies and jelly sharks. This site is good for starting a survey of favourite sweets without buying the actual sweets! Or try www.historicfood.com for the history of foods and some good pictures of banquets. www.jellyandicecreamparties.com and www.lakeland.co.uk have pictures of jelly moulds.

Some books and stories:

Don't Put Your Finger in the Jelly, Nelly; Nick Sharratt; Scholastic
Red Rockets and Rainbow Jelly; Sue Heap
Gargling with Jelly; Brian Patten; Puffin (poetry)
Smelly Jelly, Smelly Feet; Michael Rosen; Walker Books, (poetry)
Juggling a Jug of Jelly; John Foster; OUP (poetry)

Curriculum coverage grid overleaf

Potential NC KS1 Curriculum Coverage through the provocations suggested for jelly etc.

Full version of KS1 PoS on pages 69-74
Photocopiable version on page 8

Literacy

	Lit 1 speak	Lit 2 listen	Lit 3 group	Lit 4 drama	Lit 5 word	Lit 6 spell	Lit 7 text1	Lit 8 text2	Lit 9 text3	Lit10 text4	Lit11 sentence	Lit12 presentation
	1.1	2.1	3.1	4.1	5.1	6.1	7.1	8.1	9.1	10.1	11.1	12.1
	1.2	2.2	3.2	4.2	5.2	6.2	7.2	8.2	9.2	10.2	11.2	12.2

Numeracy

	Num 1 U&A	Num 2 count	Num 3 number	Num 4 calculate	Num 5 shape	Num 6 measure	Num 7 data
	1.1	2.1	3.1	4.1	5.1	6.1	7.1
	1.2	2.2	3.2	4.2	5.2	6.2	7.2

Science

	SC1 Enquiry			SC2 Life processes					SC3 Materials		SC4 Phys processes		
	Sc1.1	Sc1.2	Sc1.3	Sc2.1	Sc2.2	Sc2.3	Sc2.4	Sc2.5	Sc3.1	Sc3.2	Sc4.1	Sc4.2	Sc4.3
	1.1a	1.2a	1.3a	2.1a	2.2a	2.3a	2.4a	2.5a	3.1a	3.2a	4.1a	4.2a	4.3a
	1.1b	1.2b	1.3b	2.1b	2.2b	2.3b	2.4b	2.5b	3.1b	3.2b	4.1b	4.2b	4.3b
	1.1c	1.2c	1.3c	2.1c	2.2c	2.3c		2.5c	3.1c		4.1c	4.2c	4.3c
	1.1d				2.2d				3.1d				4.3d
					2.2e								
					2.2f								
					2.2g								

ICT

	ICT 1 finding out		ICT 2 ideas	ICT 3 reviewing	ICT 4 breadth
	1.1a	1.2a	2a	3a	4a
	1.1b	1.2b	2b	3b	4b
	1.1c	1.2c	2c	3c	4c
		1.2d			

D&T

	D&T 1 developing	D&T 2 tool use	D&T 3 evaluating	D&T 4 materials	D&T 5 breadth
	1a	2a	3a	4a	5a
	1b	2b	3b	4b	5b
	1c	2c			5c
	1d	2d			
	1e	2e			

History

	H1 chronology	H2 events, people	H3 interpret	H4 enquire	H5 org & comm	H6 breadth
	1a	2a	3a	4a	5a	6a
	1b	2b		4b		6b
						6c
						6d

Geography

	G1.1 & G1.2 enquiry		G2 places	G3 processes	G4 environment	G5 breadth
	1.1a	1.2a	2a	3a	4a	5a
	1.1b	1.2b	2b	3b	4b	5b
	1.1c	1.2c	2c			5c
	1.1d	1.2d	2d			5d
			2e			

Music

	M1 performing	M2 composing	M3 appraising	M4 listening	M5 breadth
	1a	2a	3a	4a	5a
	1b	2b	3b	4b	5b
	1c			4c	5c
					5d

PHSE & C

	PSHEC1 conf & resp	PSHEC2 citizenship	PSHEC3 health	PSHEC4 relationships
	1a	2a	3a	4a
	1b	2b	3b	4b
	1c	2c	3c	4c
	1d	2d	3d	4d
	1e	2e	3e	4e
		2f	3f	
		2g	3g	
		2h		

Art & Design

	A&D1 ideas	A&D2 making	A&D3 evaluating	A&D4 materials	A&D5 breadth
	1a	2a	3a	4a	5a
	1b	2b	3b	4b	5b
		2c		4c	5c
					5d

PE

	PE1 devel skills	PE2 apply skills	PE3 evaluate	PE4 fitness	PE5 breadth
	1a	2a	3a	4a	5a dance
	1b	2b	3b	4b	5b games
		2c	3c		5c gym

Critical skills	Thinking Skills
problem solving	observing
decision making	classifying
critical thinking	prediction
creative thinking	making inferences
communication	problem solving
organisation	drawing conclusions
management	
leadership	

Aquarium

Aquarium

Previous experience in the Foundation Stage.

Children may have already had an aquarium at home or at school. Experiences may have included:

* experimenting with model fish and plastic plants to make a model aquarium for small world play;
* using small world sea life treasures in water play;
* watching video and film of underwater stories - real life and fictional;
* visiting sea-life centres with their setting or their family;
* watching fish and other sea creatures in aquarium shops, garden centres and pet shops.

Pause for thought

In the early stages of working with these materials it is crucial to continue to observe the children. Only by doing this can you set developmentally appropriate challenges and provocations. The ideas listed here are offered as suggestions; the most exciting challenges will arise from children's own interests and motivations, which will only become apparent as you spend time with them, watching and joining them in their play. As you do this, you will be moving between the three interconnecting roles of observer, co-player, extender described below, and will be able to decide what you need to do next to take the learning forward.

The responsive adult (see page 5)

In three interconnecting roles, the responsive adult will be:

* observing
* listening
* interpreting

observer

* **modelling**
* **playing alongside**
* **offering suggestions**
* **responding sensitively**
* **initiating with care!**

co-player

* discussing ideas
* sharing thinking
* modelling new skills
* asking open questions
* being an informed extender
* instigating ideas & thoughts
* supporting children as they make links in learning
* making possibilities evident
* introducing new ideas and resources
* offering challenges and provocations

extender

Offering Challenges and Provocations - some ideas:

Cheap plastic aquarium plants and aquarium backing, with a plastic tank and some gravel will give children endless hours of play and experiment with working underwater.

? Use some plastic plants to make an aquarium in a big plastic container (a washing up bowl or bucket will do if you don't have a tank). Now add some gravel and clean stones.

? Make some fish and other sea creatures to live in your aquarium. They need to be waterproof, so use plastic or other waterproof materials, such as carrier bags, plastic food trays, egg boxes.

? Find an empty cardboard carton and tape it closed. Get an adult to help you cut an opening in one side of the box so you cab see inside. Now use the box to make an underwater scene. Paint a background inside the box, put gravel on the base, and make some plants for the aquarium. Now make some fish and hang them on cotton from the roof of the aquarium, so they look as though they are swimming. You could put clear or transparent blue plastic or cling film over the front of the aquarium to look like glass.

? Work with a friend and use books or the internet to find out about fish and other sea creatures. Use some of the images you find to make a book or presentation of what you find out.

? Can you make a model of the fish tank in the dentist's surgery in Finding Nemo? You may need to look at the DVD to remind yourself. Make the fish from card shapes, coloured with felt pens to make them bright and realistic.

? Make a story in pictures and words about a lost baby seahorse. You could use a camera to make some of the pictures.

Ready for more?

- Use the internet to find out about Sea-Life centres and big aquariums. Write to some (or email them) to see if they will send you more information.
- Look up your local pet shop or aquarium shop and see if you can visit to look at tropical and freshwater fish and other sea creatures. Ask if you can take some photos for an information book or poster for your school.
- Look at the picture of a fish tank on this page. It was made by an ice sculptor who put the tank in a block of ice, without hurting the fish! How do you think the Ice Chef did it? You could email him on charles@icechef.com to ask him. You could also look at www.icechef.com to see some more ice sculptures and some pictures of the Ice Chef showing some children how he carves ice figures.
- Work as a class to make a human sized aquarium in the corner of your room. You could hang paper weeds from the ceiling and make rocks with papier mache. Put some blue fabric on the floor and paint a big background picture with fish, sharks and other sea creatures. Go swimmimg!
- Find out which is the largest sea creature in the world. How big is it? Can you find a picture of it? Now find out about the smallest sea creatures. What do they look like? Try www.animals.nationalgeographic.co.uk to find pictures of all sorts of sea creatures.

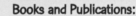
A fish tank in a block of ice!

Materials, equipment suppliers, websites, books and other references

Resources:
You will need some containers to use as aquariums - either plastic fish tanks, big jars or plastic bottles, or cardboard boxes for 'no water' aquarium scenes. Fish tanks and bowls are reasonable prices from aquarium shops, and you can add plants, rocks and stones as well as plastic or real fish. Pound shops are also good places to look for aquarium items.

Google images: 'aquarium' 'aquarium as art' 'fish sculptures' 'fishing' 'diver' 'crustaceans' 'tropical fish' 'underwater animals' 'river' 'seaside' 'underwater plants'.
and **Google web search** for information on sea life centres and aquariums in the UK and abroad:
www.national-aquarium.co.uk with photos, and a tour of the building in Plymouth
www.londonaquarium.co.uk click to the Kids Zone to find facts, and a virtual visit
www.aquariumsonline.eu for Biorb aquariums
www.ticket-centre.co.uk/sea-life-centre and click through to UK Sea Life Centres
www.sealifeeurope.com has activity pages
www.bluereefaquarium.co.uk has good fish pictures on the home page
The Deep is the award winning aquarium in Hull, East Yorkshire, which features over 3500 fish and 40 sharks www.thedeep.co.uk
www.sheddaquarium.org/oceanarium The site for the Chicago aquarium with views of exhibits.

Books and Publications:
There are so many suitable stories that we can only suggest a few here:
Rainbow Fish (and other titles by same author), Marcus Pfister; North South Books
Sharks; Jonathan Miller; Usborne
My Trip to the Aquarium; Aliki: Harper Collins
Your First Marine Aquarium; John Tullock; Barron's Educational Series
The Ocean Book; Centre For Marine Conservation; John Wiley
Captain Barnacle's Aquarium; Edward Miller; Harry N Abrahams
1001 Things to Spot in the Sea; Katie Daynes; Usborne
First Encyclopedia of Seas and Oceans; Ben Deane; Usborne
Sea-Life Art and Activities; Judy Press; Williamson Publishing
The Seaside (Curriculum Links); Suzanne Kirk; Scholastic
Seaside Scientist; Mick Manning; Franklin Watts

Curriculum coverage grid overleaf

Potential NC KS1 Curriculum Coverage through the provocations suggested for Aquarium.

Literacy

	Lit 1 speak	Lit 2 listen	Lit 3 group	Lit 4 drama	Lit 5 word	Lit 6 spell	Lit 7 text1	Lit 8 text2	Lit 9 text3	Lit10 text4	Lit11 sentence	Lit12 presentation
Literacy	1.1	2.1	3.1	4.1	5.1	6.1	7.1	8.1	9.1	10.1	11.1	12.1
	1.2	2.2	3.2	4.2	5.2	6.2	7.2	8.2	9.2	10.2	11.2	12.2

Numeracy

	Num 1 U&A	Num 2 count	Num 3 number	Num 4 calculate	Num 5 shape	Num 6 measure	Num 7 data
Numeracy	1.1	2.1	3.1	4.1	5.1	6.1	7.1
	1.2	2.2	3.2	4.2	5.2	6.2	7.2

Science

	SC1 Enquiry			SC2 Life processes					SC3 Materials		SC4 Phys processes		
	Sc1.1	Sc1.2	Sc1.3	Sc2.1	Sc2.2	Sc2.3	Sc2.4	Sc2.5	Sc3.1	Sc3.2	Sc4.1	Sc4.2	Sc4.3
Science	1.1a	1.2a	1.3a	2.1a	2.2a	2.3a	2.4a	2.5a	3.1a	3.2a	4.1a	4.2a	4.3a
	1.1b	1.2b	1.3b	2.1b	2.2b	2.3b	2.4b	2.5b	3.1b	3.2b	4.1b	4.2b	4.3b
	1.1c	1.2c	1.3c	2.1c	2.2c	2.3c		2.5c	3.1c		4.1c	4.2c	4.3c
	1.1d				2.2d				3.1d				4.3d
					2.2e								
					2.2f								
					2.2g								

ICT

	ICT 1 finding out		ICT 2 ideas	ICT 3 reviewing	ICT 4 breadth
ICT	1.1a	1.2a	2a	3a	4a
	1.1b	1.2b	2b	3b	4b
	1.1c	1.2c	2c	3c	4c
		1.2d			

Full version of KS1 PoS on pages 69-74
Photocopiable version on page 8

D&T

	D&T 1 developing	D&T 2 tool use	D&T 3 evaluating	D&T 4 materials	D&T 5 breadth
D&T	1a	2a	3a	4a	5a
	1b	2b	3b	4b	5b
	1c	2c			5c
	1d	2d			
	1e	2e			

History

	H1 chronology	H2 events, people	H3 interpret	H4 enquire	H5 org & comm	H6 breadth
History	1a	2a	3a	4a	5a	6a
	1b	2b		4b		6b
						6c
						6d

Geography

	G1.1 & G1.2 enquiry		G2 places	G3 processes	G4 environment	G5 breadth
Geography	1.1a	1.2a	2a	3a	4a	5a
	1.1b	1.2b	2b	3b	4b	5b
	1.1c	1.2c	2c			5c
	1.1d	1.2d	2d			5d
			2e			

Music

	M1 performing	M2 composing	M3 appraising	M4 listening	M5 breadth
Music	1a	2a	3a	4a	5a
	1b	2b	3b	4b	5b
	1c			4c	5c
					5d

PHSE & C

	PSHEC1 conf & resp	PSHEC2 citizenship	PSHEC3 health	PSHEC4 relationships
PHSE & C	1a	2a	3a	4a
	1b	2b	3b	4b
	1c	2c	3c	4c
	1d	2d	3d	4d
	1e	2e	3e	4e
		2f	3f	
		2g	3g	
		2h		

Art & Design

	A&D1 ideas	A&D2 making	A&D3 evaluating	A&D4 materials	A&D5 breadth
Art & Design	1a	2a	3a	4a	5a
	1b	2b	3b	4b	5b
		2c		4c	5c
					5d

PE

	PE1 devel skills	PE2 apply skills	PE3 evaluate	PE4 fitness	PE5 breadth
PE	1a	2a	3a	4a	5a dance
	1b	2b	3b	4b	5b games
		2c	3c		5c gym

Critical skills	Thinking Skills
problem solving	observing
decision making	classifying
critical thinking	prediction
creative thinking	making inferences
communication	problem solving
organisation	drawing conclusions
management	
leadership	

On the surface

On the surface

Previous experience in the Foundation Stage.

During their time in the Foundation Stage children will have experienced and experimented with floating and sinking activities in:

* free play indoors and outside, in water;
* by exploring what happens when objects are put in water;
* in the bath at home:
* when washing up after cooking and other food activities
* by looking at video and film about boats and water;
* in swimmimg pools;
* in structured, adult led activities.

Pause for thought

In the early stages of working with these materials it is crucial to continue to observe the children. Only by doing this can you set developmentally appropriate challenges and provocations. The ideas listed here are offered as suggestions; the most exciting challenges will arise from children's own interests and motivations, which will only become apparent as you spend time with them, watching and joining them in their play. As you do this, you will be moving between the three interconnecting roles of observer, co-player, extender described below, and will be able to decide what you need to do next to take the learning forward.

The responsive adult (see page 5)

In three interconnecting roles, the responsive adult will be:

observer

* observing
* listening
* interpreting

co-player

* **modelling**
* **playing alongside**
* **offering suggestions**
* **responding sensitively**
* **initiating with care!**

extender

* discussing ideas
* sharing thinking
* modelling new skills
* asking open questions
* being an informed extender
* instigating ideas & thoughts
* supporting children as they make links in learning
* making possibilities evident
* introducing new ideas and resources
* offering challenges and provocations

Offering Challenges and Provocations - some ideas:

In these challenges and provocations, we have concentrated on the surface of water. Of course, children will also be involved in the sinking aspect as they work. Much water play in the Foundation Stage may have been child initiated, and children may need to be helped to focus on a specific challenge.

? Collect 10 waterproof objects from around the room. Now find out if they will float on the surface of water in a bowl or other container. Record what you find out. What happens if you leave the objects in the water for one hour? Does anything change?

? Now can you use what you found out to collect more objects that will float. Do you notice anything similar about the objects that float? Use a camera to help you record what you find.

? Cut some circles from polystyrene or plastic containers. Can you make these float on the top of the water? Try loading the circles with counters. How many can a circle carry before it sinks? Try with different sizes.

? Collect some leaves and float them on the surface of a transparent container of water (such as a plastic aquarium). Now look at the underneath of these flat objects as they float. What can you see? Do different leaves look different? Why could this be?

? Get some cooking oil in a small container. Mix it with a few drops of food colouring if you have some. Now use a dropper or a spoon to drop small amounts of the oil on top of a bowl of water. What happens? Take some photos of your experiment.

? Get some yellow bath ducks (or other bath toys) and find out why they float. Sometimes these toys sink. Why does this happen?

? Experiment with some small water bottles. Can you make them float?

Ready for more?

- Continue your experiments with an empty water bottle. Can you make it float upright in the water? Can you make it float upside down?

- Find out about water boat-men. How do they stay afloat on the surface of the water? Can you find any other insects that can do this?

- Use the internet or a book to find out about marbling. Collect what you need and see if you can do it. Why does the ink stay on top of the water? Why doesn't it mix with the water? When your marbled paper is dry, use it to cover a display board, make a card or cover a book.

- Use the internet to find www.kids-science-experiments.com and try some of these experiments: Swimming Fish, Speedboat Matchsticks, Run Away Pepper and Bubbles. They are in the 'surface tension' section. When you have tried some of the experiments, show rhem to your friends and explain how they work (it tells you on the website!)

- Find some different sorts of seeds and test them to see if they float or sink. Use a camera to record your experiments. Why do you think some seeds float?

- Buy a water hyacinth or a water lily plant from a garden centre and keep it in a bucket. How does it live? You could add a goldfish to your pond as long as you remember to feed it!

Materials, equipment suppliers, websites, books and other references

Some ideas for resources and equipment:
Simple floating experiments can be done with a range of free materials such as:

- sticks, leaves, seeds and seed pods
- feathers, coins, pieces of bark, stones and pebbles
- offcuts of plywood or pieces of driftwood
- plastic, card, paper
- small world animals and people, construction toy pieces, marbles

One of the very best sites for teachers and children is www.kathimitchell.com where you can click through to science experiments and other education and information sites across the world - you could spend a whole term here.

Other sites include www.show.me.uk is a museum and information site for children with links to many UK museums and galleries. A site with simple science experiments for young children is www.kids-science-experiments.com where you can find experiments on surface tension such as 'fish', 'speedboat matchsticks', 'run away pepper' and 'bubbles'. Loads of easy experiments without complicated resources.

Google images: 'water creatures' 'water insects' 'water boatman' 'ducks' 'swans' 'colour changing ducks'.

Water hyacinths

Books and Other Publications:
Down in the Cool of the Pool; Tony Mitton; Orchard Books
Rory and his Rock Pool Adventure; Andrew Wolffe, Kepple Publishing
In One Tidepool; Anthony Fredericks; Dawn Publications
In the Pond; Ruth Wickins; Mercury Junior
Pond and River; Steve Parker; Dorling Kindersley
What's in The Pond; Anne Hunter; Houghton Mifflin
Creating a Wildlife Pond; Dave Bevan; Ringpress Books
Tadpoles and Frogs; Anna Milbourne; Usborne
Pond Dipping; Alison Hawes; Collins
Pond and River; Steve Parker; DK
Song of the Water Boatman; Joyce Sidman; Houghton Mifflin (Non fiction book award winner)
The Web at Dragonfly Pond; Brian Ellis; Dawn Publications
Turtle Splash; Cathryn Falwell; Greenwillow Books
Christmas at Long Pond; William T George; HarperTrophy

Curriculum coverage grid overleaf

Full version of KS1 PoS on pages 69-74
Photocopiable version on page 8

Literacy

	Lit 1 speak	Lit 2 listen	Lit 3 group	Lit 4 drama	Lit 5 word	Lit 6 spell	Lit 7 text1	Lit 8 text2	Lit 9 text3	Lit10 text4	Lit11 sentence	Lit12 presentation
	1.1	2.1	3.1	4.1	5.1	6.1	7.1	8.1	9.1	10.1	11.1	12.1
	1.2	2.2	3.2	4.2	5.2	6.2	7.2	8.2	9.2	10.2	11.2	12.2

Numeracy

	Num 1 U&A	Num 2 count	Num 3 number	Num 4 calculate	Num 5 shape	Num 6 measure	Num 7 data
	1.1	2.1	3.1	4.1	5.1	6.1	7.1
	1.2	2.2	3.2	4.2	5.2	6.2	7.2

Science

	SC1 Enquiry			SC2 Life processes					SC3 Materials		SC4 Phys processes		
	Sc1.1	Sc1.2	Sc1.3	Sc2.1	Sc2.2	Sc2.3	Sc2.4	Sc2.5	Sc3.1	Sc3.2	Sc4.1	Sc4.2	Sc4.3
	1.1a	1.2a	1.3a	2.1a	2.2a	2.3a	2.4a	2.5a	3.1a	3.2a	4.1a	4.2a	4.3a
	1.1b	1.2b	1.3b	2.1b	2.2b	2.3b	2.4b	2.5b	3.1b	3.2b	4.1b	4.2b	4.3b
	1.1c	1.2c	1.3c	2.1c	2.2c	2.3c		2.5c	3.1c		4.1c	4.2c	4.3c
	1.1d				2.2d				3.1d				4.3d
					2.2e								
					2.2f								
					2.2g								

ICT

	ICT 1 finding out	ICT 2 ideas	ICT 3 reviewing	ICT 4 breadth
	1.1a	1.2a	2a	3a	4a
	1.1b	1.2b	2b	3b	4b
	1.1c	1.2c	2c	3c	4c
		1.2d			

D&T

	D&T 1 developing	D&T 2 tool use	D&T 3 evaluating	D&T 4 materials	D&T 5 breadth
	1a	2a	3a	4a	5a
	1b	2b	3b	4b	5b
	1c	2c			5c
	1d	2d			
	1e	2e			

History

	H1 chronology	H2 events, people	H3 interpret	H4 enquire	H5 org & comm	H6 breadth
	1a	2a	3a	4a	5a	6a
	1b	2b		4b		6b
						6c
						6d

Geography

	G1.1 & G1.2 enquiry		G2 places	G3 processes	G4 environment	G5 breadth
	1.1a	1.2a	2a	3a	4a	5a
	1.1b	1.2b	2b	3b	4b	5b
	1.1c	1.2c	2c			5c
	1.1d	1.2d	2d			5d
			2e			

Music

	M1 performing	M2 composing	M3 appraising	M4 listening	M5 breadth
	1a	2a	3a	4a	5a
	1b	2b	3b	4b	5b
	1c			4c	5c
					5d

PHSE & C

	PSHEC1 conf & resp	PSHEC2 citizenship	PSHEC3 health	PSHEC4 relationships
	1a	2a	3a	4a
	1b	2b	3b	4b
	1c	2c	3c	4c
	1d	2d	3d	4d
	1e	2e	3e	4e
		2f	3f	
		2g	3g	
		2h		

Art & Design

	A&D1 ideas	A&D2 making	A&D3 evaluating	A&D4 materials	A&D5 breadth
	1a	2a	3a	4a	5a
	1b	2b	3b	4b	5b
		2c		4c	5c
					5d

PE

	PE1 devel skills	PE2 apply skills	PE3 evaluate	PE4 fitness	PE5 breadth
	1a	2a	3a	4a	5a dance
	1b	2b	3b	4b	5b games
		2c	3c		5c gym

Critical skills	Thinking Skills
problem solving	observing
decision making	classifying
critical thinking	prediction
creative thinking	making inferences
communication	problem solving
organisation	drawing conclusions
management	
leadership	

Waterproofing

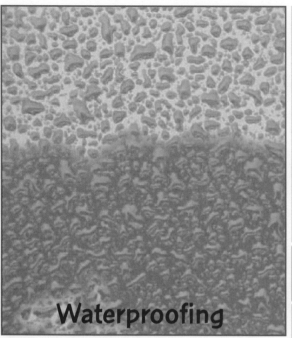

Waterproofing

Previous experience in the Foundation Stage.
Children will have had experience of water-proofing and protection from water in activities such as:

* during water play;
* when watering plants in the garden;
* when discussing protective clothing to wear out of doors and on visits;
* talking about the purpose of wearing aprons when washing things out of doors or using wet and messy materials indoors;
* making sure surfaces and objects are protected from water by covering them with waterproof materials.

Pause for thought

In the early stages of working with these materials it is crucial to continue to observe the children. Only by doing this can you set developmentally appropriate challenges and provocations. The ideas listed here are offered as suggestions; the most exciting challenges will arise from children's own interests and motivations, which will only become apparent as you spend time with them, watching and joining them in their play. As you do this, you will be moving between the three interconnecting roles of observer, co-player, extender described below, and will be able to decide what you need to do next to take the learning forward.

The responsive adult (see page 5)

In three interconnecting roles, the responsive adult will be:

* observing
* listening
* interpreting

observer

* **modelling**
* **playing alongside**
* **offering suggestions**
* **responding sensitively**
* **initiating with care!**

co-player

* discussing ideas
* sharing thinking
* modelling new skills
* asking open questions
* being an informed extender
* instigating ideas & thoughts
* supporting children as they make links in learning
* making possibilities evident
* introducing new ideas and resources
* offering challenges and provocations

extender

Offering Challenges and Provocations - some ideas:

Provide a wide range of materials for children to test and explore. Let them use these in free exploration before setting challenges.

? Collect some materials to test for water-proofness. Find a fair way of testing each material. Record your findings in a graph or chart, so it is easy to see which materials are waterproof and which are not waterproof.

? Design and make some waterproof clothes for a doll, soft toy or puppet.

? Put a small toy or teddy in a cardboard box. now make the box completely waterproof. Leave it submerged in water overnight to test how well it works - don't forget to rescue the toy and dry it out!

? Try the same experiment with different containers and different methods of waterproofing. Put porridge oats, Smarties or biscuits in the containers before waterproofing them.

? Waterproof a cardboard box and fill it full of 'treasure'. Submerge your treasure chest in water and see what happens.

? Collect some plastic carrier bags and use these to waterproof something. Use JUST THE CARRIER BAGS, NO TAPE, GLUE OR STRING! Are some bags better than others? Is it possible to make something waterproof using ONLY plastic bags?

? Find some waterproof gloves and footwear. What makes them special? Why are they waterproof? Can you design other ways of keeping your feet and hands dry? Try making what you have designed and trying it out.

? Get some thin plastic sheeting (plastic dustsheets are cheap and easy to use). Can you make a waterproof shelter with plastic sheeting and canes or sticks?

Ready for more?

- Find out how you could use wax to make something water proof. Candles or crayons are good starting points.
- Look at varnishes. How do they work to protect things from water. Use the internet to find out how they work and all the different sorts you can buy. You could try some water based varnishes, or varnish things with PVA glue. What are the problems with water based varnish?
- Can you make small objects (Lego pieces, marbles or pasta shapes) completely water-proofed by enclosing them in Plasticene or Blutack? Test what you have done.
- Collect some natural materials (feathers, leaves, bark, shells, pebbles etc). Use coloured water and a dropper to find out which ones are waterproof.
- Make a small pond outside. Find out how to stop the pond leaking. Explore 'pond liners' on the internet, and try to find out how people made ponds before there were pond liners. If possible, look at natural ponds and puddles for clues.
- Use a range of plastic materials - bin bags, carrier bags, plastic sheeting - to make your own waterproof clothing. Test it in the rain or with sprays.
- Explore how umbrellas work, and try making one yourself from sticks and plastic or waterproof fabric.

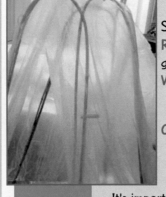

Materials, equipment suppliers, websites, books and other references

Some ideas for resources and equipment:

Recycled materials are free, so make sure the children have plenty of choice and can get the things they want to use as they work with waterproofing experiments.

Why not put a notice up inviting offers of CLEAN recycled materials such as:

- plastic bottles and tops, containers, cups, tubs and pots
- old waterproof clothing such as raincoats, boots and leggings

Collect some cheap items for experiments:

- umbrellas (adult and children's), watering cans and sprays; duct and masking tapes (from 'Pound' shops); string, wool, soft wire, cord and rope; scraps of fabric, plastic bags, plastic sheeting, bubble wrap to make trial clothes and structures

It's important to give children plenty of time to work on their projects and to find some way of protecting **unfinished projects and tests, indoors and outside**, particularly if you are expecting them to photograph the experiments for a book or presentation.

Google images: try putting words such as 'tarpaulin' 'tent' 'shelter' 'bubble wrap' 'souwester' 'oilskin' 'water collector' for images to inspire their work. and Google web for www.allplas.co.uk for plastic covers, tarpaulins, bubble-wrap, greenhouse insulation, polythene sheeting and much, much more.

At www.showplace.uk.com the Gallery has lots of examples of weatherproof structures. Or try Olympic Games sites for buildings with sliding roofs and waterproof structures - www.london2012.com www.olympics.org.uk

Books and Publications:

Wet Play Today 5-7; Andrew Brodie; Andrew Brodie Publications
Wild About the Weather; 50 wet activities; Ed Brotak; Lark Books;
Tell Me Why Rain is Wet; Shirley Willis; Book House
Wet World; Norma Simon; Candlewick Press
Plastic Raincoat (Our Clothes); Wayne Jackman; Hodder
The Tent; Dorothy Mills; Bookman Publishing
Camp Out!; Lynne Brunelle; Workman Publishing
Plastic; Henry Pluckrose; Franklin Watts
Working with Materials; C Chapman; Collins
How We Use Plastic; Chris Oxlade; Raintree
Plastic (Science Explorers); Nicola Edwards; A & C Black

Curriculum coverage grid overleaf

Potential NC KS1 Curriculum Coverage through the provocations suggested for waterproofing.

Literacy

	Lit 1 speak	Lit 2 listen	Lit 3 group	Lit 4 drama	Lit 5 word	Lit 6 spell	Lit 7 text1	Lit 8 text2	Lit 9 text3	Lit10 text4	Lit11 sentence	Lit12 presentation
Literacy	1.1	2.1	3.1	4.1	5.1	6.1	7.1	8.1	9.1	10.1	11.1	12.1
	1.2	2.2	3.2	4.2	5.2	6.2	7.2	8.2	9.2	10.2	11.2	12.2

Numeracy

	Num 1 U&A	Num 2 count	Num 3 number	Num 4 calculate	Num 5 shape	Num 6 measure	Num 7 data
Numeracy	1.1	2.1	3.1	4.1	5.1	6.1	7.1
	1.2	2.2	3.2	4.2	5.2	6.2	7.2

Full version of KS1 PoS on pages 69-74
Photocopiable version on page 8

Science

	SC1 Enquiry			SC2 Life processes					SC3 Materials		SC4 Phys processes		
	Sc1.1	Sc1.2	Sc1.3	Sc2.1	Sc2.2	Sc2.3	Sc2.4	Sc2.5	Sc3.1	Sc3.2	Sc4.1	Sc4.2	Sc4.3
Science	1.1a	1.2a	1.3a	2.1a	2.2a	2.3a	2.4a	2.5a	3.1a	3.2a	4.1a	4.2a	4.3a
	1.1b	1.2b	1.3b	2.1b	2.2b	2.3b	2.4b	2.5b	3.1b	3.2b	4.1b	4.2b	4.3b
	1.1c	1.2c	1.3c	2.1c	2.2c	2.3c		2.5c	3.1c		4.1c	4.2c	4.3c
	1.1d				2.2d				3.1d				4.3d
					2.2e								
					2.2f								
					2.2g								

ICT

	ICT 1 finding out		ICT 2 ideas	ICT 3 reviewing	ICT 4 breadth
ICT	1.1a	1.2a	2a	3a	4a
	1.1b	1.2b	2b	3b	4b
	1.1c	1.2c	2c	3c	4c
		1.2d			

D&T

	D&T 1 developing	D&T 2 tool use	D&T 3 evaluating	D&T 4 materials	D&T 5 breadth
D&T	1a	2a	3a	4a	5a
	1b	2b	3b	4b	5b
	1c	2c			5c
	1d	2d			
	1e	2e			

History

	H1 chronology	H2 events, people	H3 interpret	H4 enquire	H5 org & comm	H6 breadth
History	1a	2a	3a	4a	5a	6a
	1b	2b		4b		6b
						6c
						6d

Geography

	G1.1 & G1.2 enquiry		G2 places	G3 processes	G4 environment	G5 breadth
Geography	1.1a	1.2a	2a	3a	4a	5a
	1.1b	1.2b	2b	3b	4b	5b
	1.1c	1.2c	2c			5c
	1.1d	1.2d	2d			5d
			2e			

Music

	M1 performing	M2 composing	M3 appraising	M4 listening	M5 breadth
Music	1a	2a	3a	4a	5a
	1b	2b	3b	4b	5b
	1c			4c	5c
					5d

PHSE & C

	PSHEC1 conf & resp	PSHEC2 citizenship	PSHEC3 health	PSHEC4 relationships
PHSE & C	1a	2a	3a	4a
	1b	2b	3b	4b
	1c	2c	3c	4c
	1d	2d	3d	4d
	1e	2e	3e	4e
		2f	3f	
		2g	3g	
		2h		

Art & Design

	A&D1 ideas	A&D2 making	A&D3 evaluating	A&D4 materials	A&D5 breadth
Art & Design	1a	2a	3a	4a	5a
	1b	2b	3b	4b	5b
		2c		4c	5c
					5d

PE

	PE1 devel skills	PE2 apply skills	PE3 evaluate	PE4 fitness	PE5 breadth
PE	1a	2a	3a	4a	5a dance
	1b	2b	3b	4b	5b games
		2c	3c		5c gym

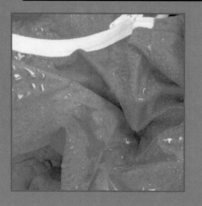

Critical skills	Thinking Skills
problem solving	observing
decision making	classifying
critical thinking	prediction
creative thinking	making inferences
communication	problem solving
organisation	drawing conclusions
management	
leadership	

The following pages contain the detail for the curriculum key which appears at the end of each section of the book. The appendix consists of the following:

1. Short-hand versions of the QCA/DfES Programme of Study for Key Stage 1 in:

   Science

   Information & Communication Technology

   Design and Technology

   History

   Geography

   Music

   Art and Design

   Physical Education

2. The suggested programme of study for Personal, Social and Health Education and Citizenship (PSHE & C)

3. The elements of the guidance for learning and teaching of Literacy and Numeracy in Years 1 and 2 (from the Primary Framework for literacy and mathematics; DfES/SureStart; Sept 2006; Ref: 02011-2006BOK-EN)

Literacy 1 speaking	Literacy 2 listening & responding	Literacy 3 group discussion & interaction	Literacy 4 drama	Literacy 5 word recognition, coding & decoding	Literacy 6 word structure & spelling	Literacy 7 understanding & interpreting texts	Literacy 8 engaging & responding to text	Literacy 9 creating and shaping texts	Literacy 10 text structure & organisation	Literacy 11 sentence structure & punctuation	Literacy 12 presentation
Year 1 **Tell stories and describe incidents** from their own experience in an audible voice **Retell stories**, ordering events using story language Interpret a text by reading aloud with some variety in pace and emphasis **Experiment with & build new stores of words** to communicate in different contexts	**Year 1** Listen with sustained concentration, building new stores of words in different contexts **Listen to and follow instructions** accurately, asking for help and clarification if necessary Listen to tapes or video and express views about how a story or information has been presented	**Year 1** **Take turns to speak, listen to** others' suggestions and talk about what they are going to do Ask and answer questions, make relevant contributions, offer suggestions and take turns **Explain their views to others** in a small group, decide how to report the group's views to the class	**Year 1** Explore familiar themes and characters through improvisation and role-play **Act out their own and well-known stories**, using voices for characters Discuss why they like a performance	**Year 1** **Recognise & use alternative ways of pronouncing the graphemes already taught**, for example, that the grapheme 'g' is pronounced differently in 'get' and 'gem'; the grapheme 'ow' is pronounced differently in 'how' & 'show' **Recognise and use alternative ways of spelling the phonemes already taught**, for example 'ae' ' can be spelt with 'ai', 'ay' or 'a-e'; begin to know which words contain which spelling alternatives **Identify the constituent parts of two-syllable and three-syllable words** to support the application of phonic knowledge and skills Recognise automatically an increasing number of familiar high frequency words **Apply phonic knowledge & skills** as the prime approach to reading & spelling unfamiliar words that are not completely decodable **Read more challenging texts** which can be decoded using their acquired phonic knowledge & skills; automatic recognition of high frequency words Read and spell phonically decodable two-syllable and three-syllable words	**Year 1** Spell new words using phonics as the prime approach Segment sounds into their constituent phonemes in order to spell them correctly Children move from spelling simple CVC words to longer words that include common digraphs & adjacent consonants such as 'brush', 'crunch' **Recognise & use alternative ways of spelling the graphemes already taught**, for example that the /ae/ sound can be spelt with 'ai', 'ay' or 'a-e'; that the /ee/ sound can also be spelt as 'ea' and 'e'; & begin to know which words contain which spelling alternatives Use knowledge of common inflections in spelling, such as plurals, -ly, -er **Read & spell phonically decodable 2- & 3 syllable words**	**Year 1** **Identify the main events and characters in stories**, and find specific information in simple texts Use syntax and context when reading for meaning **Make predictions** showing an understanding of ideas, events and characters Recognise the main elements that shape different texts **Explore the effect of patterns of language &** repeated words & phrases	**Year 1** Select books for personal reading and give reasons for choices **Visualise and comment on** events, characters and ideas, making imaginative links to their own experiences Distinguish fiction and non-fiction texts and the different purposes for reading them	**Year 1** **Independently choose what to write about**, plan and follow it through Use key features of narrative in their own writing Convey information and ideas in simple non-narrative forms **Find and use new and interesting words and phrases**, including story language **Create short simple texts** on paper and on screen that combine words with images (and sounds)	**Year 1** Write chronological and non-chronological texts using simple structures **Group written sentences together in chunks** of meaning or subject	**Year 1** **Compose and write simple sentences independently** to communicate meaning Use capital letters and full stops when punctuating simple sentences	**Year 1** Write most letters, correctly formed and orientated, using a comfortable and efficient pencil grip **Write with spaces between words accurately** Use the space bar and keyboard to type their name & simple texts
Year 2 Speak with clarity and use appropriate intonation when reading and reciting texts **Tell real and imagined stories** using the conventions of familiar story language Explain ideas and processes using imaginative and adventurous vocabulary and non-verbal gestures to support communication	**Year 2** Listen to others in class, ask relevant questions and follow instructions Listen to talk by an adult, remember some specific points and identify what they have learned **Respond to presentations** by describing characters, repeating some highlight and commenting constructively	**Year 2** Ensure that everyone contributes, allocate tasks, and consider alternatives and reach agreement **Work effectively in groups** by ensuring that each group member takes a turn challenging, supporting and moving on Listen to each other's views and preferences, agree the next steps to take and identify contributions by each group member	**Year 2** Adopt appropriate roles in small or large groups and consider alternative courses of action Present part of traditional stories, their own stories or work drawn from different parts of the curriculum for members of their own class **Consider how mood and atmosphere are created** in live or recorded performance	**Year 2** Read independently and with increasing fluency longer and less familiar texts **Spell with increasing accuracy and confidence**, drawing on word recognition and knowledge of word structure, and spelling patterns Know how to tackle unfamiliar words that are not completely decodable **Read and spell less common alternative graphemes** including trigraphs Read high and medium frequency words independently and automatically	**Year 2** **Spell with increasing accuracy** and confidence, drawing on word recognition and knowledge of word structure, spelling patterns including common inflections and use of double letters Read and spell less common alternative graphemes including trigraphs **Understanding and interpreting texts**	**Year 2** Draw together ideas & information from across a whole text, using simple signposts in the text **Give reasons why things happen or characters change** Explain organisational features of texts, including alphabetical order, layout, diagrams etc **Use syntax & context** to build their store of vocabulary when reading Explore how particular words are used, including words & expressions with similar meanings	**Year 2** **Read whole books on their own**, choosing and justifying selections Engage with books through exploring and enacting interpretations **Explain their reactions to texts**, commenting on important aspects	**Year 2** Draw on knowledge and experience of texts in deciding and planning what & how to write **Sustain form in narrative**, including use of person & time Maintain consistency in non-narrative, including purpose & tense **Make adventurous word and language choices** appropriate to the style and purpose of the text **Select from different presentational features** to suit particular writing purposes on paper & on screen	**Year 2** Use planning to establish clear sections for writing Use appropriate language to make sections hang together	**Year 2** Write simple and compound sentences and begin to use subordination in relation to time and reason **Compose sentences using tense consistently** (present & past) Use question marks, and use commas to separate items in a list	**Year 2** Write legibly, using upper and lower case letters appropriately within words, and observing correct spacing within and between words Form and use the four basic handwriting joins **Word process short narrative** and non-narrative texts

NC KS1 Programme of Study - Literacy
(revised framework objectives)

Numeracy 1	Numeracy 2	Numeracy 3	Numeracy 4	Numeracy 5	Numeracy 6	Numeracy 7
using and applying mathematics	counting & understanding number	knowing & using number facts	calculating	understanding shape	measuring	handling data
Year 1	**Year 1**	**Year 1**	**Year 1**	**Year 1**	**Year 1**	**Year 1**
Solve problems involving counting, adding, subtracting, doubling or halving in the context of numbers, measures or money, for example to 'pay' & 'give change' **Describe a puzzle or problem** using numbers, practical materials & diagrams; use these to solve the problem & set the solution in the original context **Answer a question** by selecting and using suitable equipment, and sorting information, shapes or objects; display results using tables and pictures **Describe simple patterns** and relationships involving numbers or shapes; decide whether examples satisfy given conditions **Describe ways of solving puzzles** and problems, explaining choices and decisions orally or using pictures	**Count reliably at least 20 objects**, recognising that when rearranged the number of objects stays the same; estimate a number of objects that can be checked by counting **Compare and order numbers,** using the related vocabulary; use the equals (=) sign **Read and write numerals from 0 to 20**, then beyond; use knowledge of place value to position these numbers on a number track and number line **Say the number that is 1 more or less than any given number, & 10 more or less for multiples of 10** **Use the vocabulary of halves and quarters in context**	Derive and recall all pairs of numbers with a total of 10 and addition facts for totals to at least 5; work out the corresponding subtraction facts **Count on or back in ones, twos, fives and tens** and use this knowledge to derive the multiples of 2, 5 and 10 to the tenth multiple Recall the doubles of all numbers to at least 10	**Relate addition to counting on;** recognise that addition can be done in any order; use practical and informal written methods to support the addition of a one-digit number or a multiple of 10 to a one-digit or two-digit number Understand subtraction as 'take away' and find a 'difference' by counting up; use practical and informal written methods to support the subtraction of a one-digit number from a one-digit or two-digit number and a multiple of 10 from a two-digit number **Use the vocabulary related to addition and subtraction and symbols** to describe and record addition and subtraction number sentences Solve practical problems that involve combining groups of 2, 5 or 10, or sharing into equal groups	Visualise and name common 2-D shapes and 3-D solids and describe their features; use them to make patterns, pictures & models **Identify objects that turn about a point** (e.g. scissors) or about a line (e.g. a door); recognise & make whole, half & quarter turns Visualise & use everyday language to describe the position of objects and direction and distance when moving them, for example when placing or moving objects on a game board	**Estimate, measure, weigh and compare objects,** choosing & using suitable uniform non-standard or standard units & measuring instruments (e.g. a lever balance, metre stick or measuring jug) Use vocabulary related to time; order days of the week & months; read the time to the hour & half hour	Answer a question by recording information in lists & tables; present outcomes using practical resources, pictures, block graphs or pictograms **Use diagrams to sort objects into groups** according to a given criterion; suggest a different criterion for grouping the same objects
Year 2	**Year 2**	**Year 2**	**Year 2**	**Year 2**	**Year 2**	**Year 2**
Solve problems involving addition, subtraction, multiplication or division in contexts of numbers, measures or pounds and pence **Identify and record the information or calculation needed to solve a puzzle or problem**; carry out the steps or calculations and check the solution in the context of the problem **Follow a line of enquiry;** answer questions by choosing and using suitable equipment and selecting, organising and presenting information in lists, tables and simple diagrams **Describe patterns and relationships** involving numbers or shapes, make predictions and test these with examples Present solutions to puzzles and problems in an organised way; explain decisions, methods and results in pictorial, spoken or written form, using mathematical language and number sentences	**Read and write two-digit and three-digit numbers in figures and words;** describe and extend number sequences and recognise odd and even numbers Count up to 100 objects by grouping them and counting in tens, fives or twos; explain what each digit in a two-digit number represents, including numbers where 0 is a place holder; partition two-digit numbers in different ways, including into multiples of 10 and 1 **Order two-digit numbers** and position them on a number line; use the greater than (>) and less than (<) signs **Estimate a number of objects;** round two-digit numbers to the nearest 10 Find one half, one quarter and three quarters of shapes and sets of objects	Derive and recall all addition and subtraction facts for each number to at least 10, all pairs with totals to 20 and all pairs of multiples of 10 with totals up to 100 **Understand that halving is the inverse of doubling and derive and recall doubles of all numbers to 20, and the corresponding halves** Derive and recall multiplication facts for the 2, 5 and 10 times-tables and the related division facts; recognise multiples of 2, 5 and 10 **Use knowledge of number facts and operations to estimate and check answers to calculations**	**Add or subtract mentally a one-digit number or a multiple of 10 to or from any two-digit number;** use practical and informal written methods to add and subtract two-digit numbers Understand that subtraction is the inverse of addition and vice versa; use this to derive and record related addition and subtraction number sentences **Represent repeated addition and arrays as multiplication,** and sharing and repeated subtraction (grouping) as division; use practical and informal written methods and related vocabulary to support multiplication and division, including calculations with remainders Use the symbols +, -, ?, ÷ and = to record and interpret number sentences involving all four operations; calculate the value of an unknown in a number sentence	Visualise common 2-D shapes and 3-D solids; identify shapes from pictures of them in different positions and orientations; sort, make and describe shapes, referring to their properties **Identify reflective symmetry in patterns and 2-D shapes** and draw lines of symmetry in shapes Follow and give instructions involving position, direction and movement **Recognise and use whole, half and quarter turns,** both clockwise and anticlockwise; know that a right angle represents a quarter turn	**Estimate, compare & measure lengths, weights and capacities,** choosing & using standard units (m, cm, kg, litre) & suitable measuring instruments Read the numbered divisions on a scale, and interpret the divisions between them (e.g. on a scale from 0 to 25 with intervals of 1 shown but only the divisions 0, 5, 10, 15 and 20 numbered); use a ruler to draw and measure lines to the nearest centimetre **Use units of time (seconds, minutes, hours, days) and know the relationships between them;** read the time to the quarter hour; identify time intervals, including those that cross the hour	Answer a question by collecting and recording data in lists and tables; represent the data as block graphs or pictograms to show results; use ICT to organise and present data **Use lists, tables and diagrams to sort objects;** explain choices using appropriate language, including 'not'

Programme of Study - Numeracy (revised framework objectives)

SC1 scientific enquiry			SC2 life processes & living things					SC3 materials and their properties		SC4 physical processes		
Sc1.1 planning	Sc1.2 ideas & evidence; collecting evidence	Sc1.3 comparing evidence	Sc2.1 life processes	Sc2.2 humans and other animals	Sc2.3 green plants	Sc2.4 variation and classification	Sc2.5 living things in their environment	Sc3.1 grouping materials	Sc3.2 changing materials	Sc4.1 electricity	Sc4.2 forces and motion	Sc4.3 light and sound
1.1a ask questions 'How?', 'Why?', 'What if?') and decide how they might find answers to them	1.2a follow simple instructions to control the risks to themselves and to others	1.3a make simple comparisons (eg, hand span, shoe size) and identify simple patterns or associations, and try to explain it, drawing on their knowledge and understanding	2.1a differences between things that are living and things that have never been alive	2.2a recognise and compare the main external parts of the bodies of humans and other animals	2.3a recognise that plants need light and water to grow	2.4a recognise similarities and differences between themselves and others, and to treat others with sensitivity	2.5a find out about the different kinds of plants and animals in the local environment	3.1a use their senses to explore and recognise the similarities and differences between materials	3.2a find out how the shapes of objects made from some materials can be changes by some processes, including squashing, bending, twisting & stretching	4.1a about everyday appliances that use electricity	4.2a find out about, & describe the movement of, familiar things (e.g. cars going faster, slowing down, changing direction)	4.3a identify different light sources, including the Sun
1.1b use first-hand experience & simple information sources to answer questions	1.2b explore, using the senses of sight, hearing, smell, touch & taste as appropriate, & make & record observations & measurements	1.3b compare what happened with what they expected would happen, and try to explain it. Drawing on their knowledge and understanding	2.1b that animals, including humans, move, feed, grow, use their senses and reproduce	2.2b that humans and other animals need food and water to stay alive	2.3b to recognise and name the leaf, flowers, stem and root of flowering plants	2.4b group living things according to observable similarities and differences	2.5b identify similarities & differences between local environments & ways in which these affect animals & plants that are found there	3.1b sort objects into groups on the basis of their properties texture, float, hardness, transparency & whether they are magnetic or non-magnetic)	3.2b explore & describe the way some everyday materials) for example water, chocolate, bread, clay, change when they are heated or cooled	4.1b simple series circuits involving batteries, wires, bulbs and other components - eg buzzers	4.2b that both pushes and pulls are examples of forces	4.3b that darkness is the absence of light
1.1c think about what might happen before deciding what to do	1.2c communicate what happened in a variety of ways, including using ICT	1.3c review their work and explain what they did to others	2.1c relate life processes to animals and plants found in the local environment	2.2c that taking exercise and eating the right types and amounts of food help humans to keep healthy	2.3c that seeds grow into flowering plants		2.5c care for the environment	3.1c recognise and name common types of material & recognise that some of them are found naturally		4.1c how a switch can be used to break a circuit	4.2c to recognise that when things speed up, slow down or change direction, there is a cause	4.3c that there are many kinds of sound and sources of sound
1.1d Recognise when a test or comparison is unfair				2.2d about the role of drugs as medicines				3.1d find out about the uses of a variety of materials & how these are chosen for specific uses on the basis of their simple properties				4.3d that sounds travel away from sources, getting fainter as they do so, and that they are heard
			2.2e how to treat animals with care and sensitivity									
			2.2f that humans and other animals can produce offspring and that these offspring grow into adults									
			2.2g about the senses that enable humans and other animals to be aware of the world around them									

NC KS1 Programme of Study for Key Stage 1 - Science

NC KS1 Programme of Study - ICT

ICT 1 — 1.1 finding things out / 1.2 developing ideas and making things happen		ICT 2 exchanging and sharing information	ICT 3 reviewing, modifying & evaluating work as it progresses	ICT 4 breadth of study
1.1a gather information from a variety of sources	1.2a use text, tables, images & sound to develop their ideas	2a share their ideas by presenting information in a variety of forms	3a review what they have done to help them develop their ideas	4a work with a range of information to investigate the ways it can be presented
1.1b enter & store information in a variety of forms	1.2b select from and add to information they have	2b present their completed work effectively	3b describe the effects of their actions	4b exploring a variety of ICT tools
1.1c retrieve information that has been stored	1.2c plan & give instructions to make things happen		3c talk about what they might change in future work	4c talk about the uses of ICT inside and outside school
	1.2d try things out & explore what happens in real & imaginary instructions			

NC KS1 Programme of Study - History

H1 chronological understanding	H2 K & U of events, people & changes	H3 historical interpretation	H4 historical enquiry	H5 organisation & communication	H6 breadth of study
1a place events and objects in chronological order	2a recognise why people did things, why events happened and what happened as a result	3a identify different ways in which the past is represented	4a find out about the past from a range of sources of information	5a select from their knowledge of history and communicate it in a variety of ways	6a changes in their own lives and the way of life of their family or others around them
1b use common words and phrases relating to the passing of time (for example, before, after, a long time ago, past)	2b identify differences between ways of life at different times		4b ask and answer questions about the past		6b the way of life of people in the more distant past who lived in the local area or elsewhere in Britain
					6c the lives of significant men, women and children
					6d past events from the history of Britain and the wider world

NC KS1 Programme of Study - D&T

D&T 1 developing planning & communicating ideas	D&T 2 working with tools, equipment, materials	D&T 3 evaluating processes & products	D&T 4 k & u of materials & components	D&T 5 breadth of study
1a generate ideas	2a explore sensory qualities of materials	3a talk about their ideas	4a working characteristics of materials	5a focused practical tasks
1b develop ideas	2b measure, mark out, cut and shape	3b identify improvements	4b how mechanisms can be used	5b design & make assignments
1c talk about their ideas	2c assemble, join & combine materials			5c investigate & evaluate products
1d plan what to do next	2d use simple finishing techniques			
1e communicate ideas	2e follow safe procedures			

NC KS1 Programme of Study - Geography

G1.1 & G1.2 geographical and enquiry skills		G2 knowledge & understanding of places	G3 knowledge & understanding of patterns & processes	G4 knowledge & understanding of environment	G5 breadth of study
1.1a ask geographical questions	1.2a use geographical vocabulary	2a identify & describe what places are like	3a make observations about where things are located	4a recognise changes in the environment	5a the locality of the school
1.1b observe and record	1.2b use fieldwork skills	2b identify and describe what places are	3b recognise changes in physical & human features	4b recognise how the environment may be improved & sustained	5b a contrasting locality in the UK or overseas
1.1c express their own views about people, places & environments	1.2c use globes, maps & plans at a range of scales	2c recognise how places become they way they are & how they are changing			5c study at a local scale
1.1d communicate in different ways	1.2d use secondary sources of information	2d recognise how places compare with other places			5d carry out fieldwork investigations outside the classroom
		2e recognise how places are linked to other places in the world			

Programme of Study for Key Stage 1 - Art & Design

A&D1 exploring & developing ideas	A&D2 investigating & making art, craft and design	A&D3 evaluating & developing work	A&D4 k & u of materials & components	A&D5 breadth of study
1a record from first hand observation, experience & imagination	2a investigate the possibilities of materials and processes	3a review what they and others have done	4a visual and tactile elements	5a exploring a range of starting points
1b ask and answer questions about the starting points for their work	2b try out tools & techniques & apply these	3b identify what they might change	4b materials & processes used in making art, craft & design	5b working on their own, and collaborating with others
	2c represent observations, ideas and feelings		4c differences & similarities in the work of artists, craftspeople & designers	5c using a range of materials and processes
				5d investigating different kinds of art, craft & design

Programme of Study for Key Stage 1 - Music

M1 performing skills	M2 composing skills	M3 responding & reviewing (appraising skills)	M4 responding & reviewing (listening skills)	M5 breadth of study
1a use their voices expressively by singing songs, chants, rhymes	2a create musical patterns	3a explore and express their ideas and feelings about music	4a listen with concentration & internalise & recall sounds	5a a range of musical activities
1b play tuned & untuned instruments	2b explore, choose & organise sounds & musical ideas	3b make improvements to their own work	4b how combined musical elements can be organised	5b responding to a range of starting points
1c rehearse and perform with others			4c how sounds can be made in different ways	5c working on their own, in groups & as a class
				5d a range of live and recorded music

Programme of Study for Key Stage 1 - PE

PE1 acquiring and developing skills	PE2 selecting and applying skills, tactics and compositional ideas	PE3 evaluating and improving performance	PE4 knowledge and understanding of fitness and health	PE5 breadth of study
1a explore basic skills, actions and ideas with increasing understanding	2a explore how to choose & apply skills and actions in sequence & in combination	3a describe what they have done	4a how important it is to be active	5a dance
1b remember & repeat simple skills & actions with increasing control	2b vary the way they perform skills by using simple tactics and movement phrases	3b observe, describe & copy what others have done	4b recognise & describe how their bodies feel during different activities	5b games
	2c apply rules and conventions for different activities	3c use what they have learnt to improve the quality and control of their work		5c gymnastics

Programme of Study for Key Stage 1 - PSHE

PSHEC1 developing confidence & responsibility & making the most of their abilities	PSHEC2 preparing to play an active role as citizens	PSHEC3 developing a healthier lifestyle	PSHEC4 developing good relationships & respecting differences
1a recognise their likes & dislikes, what is fair & unfair, what is right & wrong	2a take part in discussions with one other person and the whole class	3a make simple choices that improve their health & wellbeing	4a recognise how their behaviour affects other people
1b share their opinions on things that matter to them and their views	2b take part in a simple debate about topical issues	3b maintain personal hygiene	4b listen to other people and play and work co-operatively
1c recognise, name and deal with their feelings in a positive way	2c recognise choices they make, & the difference between right & wrong	3c how some diseases spread and can be controlled	4c identify and respect differences and similarities between people
1d think about themselves, learn from their experiences & recognise what they are good at	2d realise that people and other living things have needs, & that they have responsibilities to meet them	3d about the process of growing from young to old & how people's needs change	4d that family and friends should care for each other
1e how to set simple goals	2e that they belong to various groups & communities, such as a family	3e the names of the main parts of the body	4e that there are different types of teasing & bullying, that bullying is wrong
	2f what improves & harms their local, natural & built environments	3f that household products & medicines, can be harmful	
	2g contribute to the life of the class and school	3g rules for, and ways of, keeping safe, basic road safety	
	2h realise that money comes from different sources		

Credits and references

The following organisations and individuals have kindly given permission for photographs to be used in this book:
ASCO Educational

Web sites included in this book (in alphabetical order):

www.aflex-hose.co.uk for hoses of all sorts
www.aldous.co.uk Fred Aldous for dyes, batik and marbling equipment
www.allplas.co.uk for plastic covers, tarpaulins, bubble-wrap, greenhouse insulation, polythene sheeting etc
www.amazon.co.uk supply all the toy submarines shown in this book
www.aquariumsonline.eu for biorb aquariums
www.aquarterof.co.uk is a site about sweets where you can look for details of all sorts of sweets, including jelly babies and jelly sharks
www.aquaturtle.co.uk a diving school for kids
www.ascoeducational.co.uk educational supplier of toys and equipment
www.bbc.co.uk/health or ga.water.usgs.gov fact sheets on water are available on
www.blackjackbuffers.com for photos of Russian ice sculptures or
www.bluereefaquarium.co.uk has good fish pictures on the home page
www.cunard.co.uk and order a cruise brochure.
www.eduzone.co.uk Eduzone: educational supplier
www.esupply.co.uk plastic pipettes cheap in packs of 100
www.flexiblehose.co.uk www.holmeshose.co.uk - some sites with pumping and hose equipment -
www.historicfood.com for the history of foods and some good pictures of banquets.
www.hoseint.co.uk drilling platforms

www.hms-victory.com the official website for HMS Victory
www.icechef.com for some wonderful examples of ice carving and photos of the ice chef at work
www.icleinn.com where there is an ice cube scramble for kids that might be worth replicating in school!
www.jellyandicecreamparties.com have pictures of jelly moulds.
www.jorvik-viking-centre.co.uk for Vikings and their ships.
www.kathimitchell.com one of the very best sites for teachers and children is where you can click through to science experiments and other education and information sites across the world - you could spend a whole term here.
www.kids-science-experiments.com for experiments in floating and sinking
www.kidzone.ws/water has fun facts for kids about the Water Cycle
www.lakeland.co.uk get ice packs and jelly moulds here

www.liquidsculpture.com for some breathtaking images of water drops
www.londonaquarium.co.uk click to the Kids Zone to find facts and a virtual visit
www.metric.org.uk/whatis/definitions has useful conversion charts
www.national-aquarium.co.uk with photos, and a tour of the building in Plymouth

www.new.craftpacks.co.uk for measuring beakers, or ask your science co-ordinator for their suppliers

www.philipharris.co.uk for syringes, pipettes aannd tubing suitable for school use

www.pioneerthinking.com/naturaldyes which is a USA site, but has lots of information on what to use and how to prepare natural dyes

www.plumbworld.co.uk has an incredible variety of branded water pipes

www.primaryschoolscience.com/clipart has good clipart of science equipment such as beakers for displays etc - look in the Chemistry section.

www.reuk.co.uk has an explanation of how water wheels work (click through to 'hydro').

www-saps.plantsci.cam.ac for information on self watering plants

www.screwfix.com has a vast range of plumbing equipment to look at

www.sealifeeurope.com has activity pages

www.sheddaquarium.org/oceanarium the site for the Chicago aquarium with views of exhibits.

www.show.me.uk is a museum and information site for children with links to many UK museums and galleries.

www.showplace.uk.com look at the Gallery for photos

www.thedeep.co.uk The Deep is the award winning aquarium in Hull, East Yorkshire. which features over 3500 fish and 40 sharks

www.thenaturaldyestudio.com for information on natural dyes try or

www.thisisthelife.com for Ice sculptures in Alaska.

www.ticket-centre.co.uk/sea-life-centre and click through to UK Sea Life Centres

www.titanic-titanic.com, or www.historyonthenet.com for Titanic information

www.tts-group.co.uk TTS Group have a wide range of water toys and containers and food colouring in big bottles

www.wateraid.org/uk is a site for charity collections to support water aid.

www.waterwheelfactory.com or www.leahy-hill.com will take you to working water mills and a water wheel factory

www.williampye.com is a great site for water sculpture - look at 'sources of information' and the 'large and small works' sections and see 'Brimming Bowl', 'Scylla' and 'Archimedes'

www.woodlands-junior.kent.sch.uk a school site with activities and worksheets.

Carrying on in Key Stage One

Other titles in this series include:

Construction (published)

Sand (Published)

Role Play (Autumn 07)

Outdoor experiences (Autumn 07)

and

Sculpting, Stuffing and Squeezing (Winter 07)

Ring for more information on 01858 881212 or look on the website

www.featherstone.uk.com